Straight Talk About Self-care

for Human Service Workers

Dr John Ashfield PhD
© YouCanHelp Publishing 2017

For further copies of this booklet
Contact: Phone 0439 692 975 **Email:** mcrafter@youcanhelp.com.au
Graphic design: Green Pigeon Graphics – Johanna Evans
General editing: Sharon Maree Crafter

Straight Talk About Self-care

for Human Service Workers

by John Ashfield PhD

IMPORTANT NOTE

The information and ideas in this book are not intended as a substitute for medical or other forms of professional assessment, diagnosis, treatment, or therapy. Some of the information contained here will, over time, be subject to change due to advances in knowledge and changes in population health. In cases of physical or mental health difficulties, information and advice from a qualified medical practitioner should always be sought.

All responsibility for editorial matters rests with the author(s). Any views or opinions expressed or advice given are therefore not necessarily those of YouCanHelp Publishing. The information and/or self-help resources in this publication are not intended as a substitute for mental health assessment, medical or psychiatric consultation, assessment or treatment.

No part of this document can be reproduced in any way without permission of YouCanHelp whose materials are protected under law with a registered trademark.

Permission can be sought from: mcrafter@youcanhelp.com.au

Copyright protected

Contents

Preface 5

Why You Must Matter 6

How You Can Wreck Yourself by Being a 'Rescuer' 8

Setting Boundaries for Self-preservation 12

Work and Play: Achieving a Sustainable Ratio 20

Taking Care of Yourself After a Critical Incident 22

Bad Experiences Can Rub Off on You 25

Learning to Manage Stress 32

Why Self-medication is a Poor Substitute for Self-care 36

Getting Enough Exercise to Stay Healthy 46

You Are What You Eat 48

Conflict: Learning to Manage the Unavoidable 51

Meditation for in the Workplace 55

References 65

Preface

The purpose of this book is to provide human service workers and professionals with simple and practical principles and strategies for self-care. Despite being amongst the most self-giving and compassionate people in our community, those who occupy human service roles are often little considerate of themselves and their own wellbeing. It is intended that this book will be a resource that human service organisations and agencies will obtain and distribute to their employees and contractors.

In this brief volume, topics have been chosen for their immediate practical importance. Though tapping into many technical sources of 'tried and tested' ideas and data, they are presented purposely in straightforward language and with simple accompanying self-care and self-help strategies. The thought being that, busy people don't need the added stress of having to 'mine' for useful ideas in a laboured or academic style of content.

The book commences by highlighting that self-care and care for others are inseparably part of a single moral imperative of human service. It concludes with a theme that is rapidly becoming a key consideration in psychological practice, health promotion, and preventative mental health: the use of principles of meditation for self-care, general health, and wellbeing.

Why You Must Matter

Ever dressed in a hurry and in buttoning up a shirt or blouse you didn't pay enough attention and started doing up the buttons in the wrong sequence, thus, every subsequent button was done up wrongly and you had to undo them all and start again at the top?

The 'top button' of this book is to first establish *why you must matter* as a human service worker, and why valuing yourself is inseparable from the whole enterprise of effectively caring about and helping others. Actually, the two rise or fall together and must both be given due attention. If you don't grasp the fact that *you must matter*, then not much else that follows this chapter will have value for you. This, of all the chapters is the one to take your time over and read reflectively.

Most of us are drawn into human service work out of what has been termed 'altruism' - concern for others, and the endeavour in some way to help them and improve their experience; which on the face of it, seems like a virtuous and moral thing to be doing. But is it really that simple? Rarely is human service work without mixed motives, and though our heart may well be in the right place (as they say), with how much awareness do we factor ourselves into this picture? To explore *why you must matter*, we'll borrow some musings from Carl Jung, a famous Swiss psychiatrist and psychoanalyst (the two sources used are listed in the reference list).

It is widely recognised that human service work should be characterised by a deep respect for people, for the facts of their situation, and their experience of it. Jung called this a 'moral achievement'. It follows then, that if we wish to help others we need to be able to accept them as they are. But can we do this without first we have noticed and accepted ourselves? Sounds simple enough, and you've probably heard this said before. However, simple things are often the most difficult to comprehend properly.

There is virtue in caring for and helping others, but what if I stand in need of compassion, acceptance, being affirmed and valued?

What if I fail to notice and show respect for myself? How can I simply reverse the moral principle of my human service work and refuse to admit that this 'poor' person has ever crossed my path? Surely such 'selective compassion' where I choose nonchalantly to remain in ignorance about myself while being busy with other people and their troubles, is rather fraudulent? I may feel virtuous but have I deceived myself and others around me?

> There is virtue in caring for and helping others, but what if I stand in need of compassion, acceptance, being affirmed and valued? What if I fail to notice and show respect for myself?

Most of us struggle with the idea of self-acceptance and though we may in many ways do things for ourselves, even to the extent of selfishness, we fail to reflectively acknowledge our own hurts, insecurities, fears, and struggles; we do not choose to truly notice and value ourselves.

Jung suggests that we quite naturally don't want to be ourselves, instead imagining who we ought to be or would prefer to be, and making every effort not to be ourselves. This creates the idea that it is not good to be ourselves or to think of ourselves. In response to this tendency, Jung quotes from a scripture passage of Christian origin: '…love your neighbour as yourself', pointing out that we are unhesitatingly responsive to the ideal of loving our neighbour, but ignore the imperative of the same moral precept: 'as yourself'. So, we may be agreeable with the idea of loving our neighbour, but what if the neighbour that is ignored, that begs acceptance, needs nurture and kindness, happens to be ourselves?

As already stated, these two imperatives rise or fall together, because both are inseparably part of the one moral principle. Some ethicists argue that to act in a way that is truly in our best interests (selfishness is not) is at the same time in the best interests of others, and that these are intertwined in a profound yet not always immediately evident way; an idea well worth pondering.

It may be a more satisfactory rendition of *altruism*, especially if altruism is to be effective and avoid fraudulence, for it to necessarily include a genuine attempt at self-acceptance and self-compassion, as well as a genuine attempt to accept and show compassion to others. Granted, there are rare occasions in some extraordinary human lives that call for selfless heroism. But that isn't the norm, and if we are to sustain our efforts of human service over the long haul, the moral imperative of *you must matter* holds, and we'd best genuinely decide to pay attention to it.

How You Can Wreck Yourself by Being a 'Rescuer'

Many human occupations and roles, especially those of the human services or helping professions, harbour rescuers. The general list could on occasions include parents, grandparents, workplace supervisors and managers, social workers, nurses, ministers, counsellors, psychologists, mental health workers, teachers, doctors, welfare workers, just to name a few. Any of these occupations and roles potentially provide a perfect 'cover' and opportunity for rescuing.

Simply put, rescuers find it difficult to resist the temptation to jump in and try and fix other people's problems, often without clear invitation, and to a degree that is uncalled for, sometimes unwanted (though the rescued are loath to complain), and by inference communicating that *I am more competent than you and am being extra generous in going out of my way to help you to a degree that no one else has or will.*

Before you hastily discount any likelihood of this applying to you, at least be open to the possibility that it might, even to a small degree. Fortunately, it is a compulsion that can be remedied with greater awareness, self-monitoring, and some modification of choices. But let's first explore this behaviour in more detail.

You might say, "some people need to be rescued?", and you would be right, yes, they do. It would also be right to say, because some people rescue others *inappropriately* does not negate the proper use of rescuing. However, other than disaster scenes or situations which pose imminent danger to individuals, rescuing others is not usually required or desirable.

Rescuing (in the sense that it is meant here) is a behaviour that has the potential for quite negative consequences, not the least of which for the rescuer themselves. Being a rescuer runs contrary to the practice of self-valuing self-care, and tends to: develop dependence in others, exacerbate their sense of powerlessness, and deprives them of experience and initiative that may be vital to them recovering their capacity of self-efficacy. In almost all circumstances, people being helped need to be encouraged to play whatever part they can in feeling like they are in control of their lives, and experiencing a sense of autonomous personal agency.

Common negative consequences of rescuing are that, the individual being rescued may grow to resent being controlled, disempowered, and made to feel less than competent (even though the comfort of being rescued may initially be welcome). They may express emotion or an attitude that is confusing for the rescuer, or may outright reject their intrusive intervention or 'help'. Both rescuer and rescued are diminished by this experience.

> In almost all circumstances, people being helped need to be encouraged to play whatever part they can in feeling like they are in control of their lives, and experiencing a sense of autonomous personal agency.

Rescuing of this kind may not always be evident to the untrained eye, because it appears altruistic, is couched in terms that are persuasive and plausible, may initially be welcome (because the rescuer is skilled at bringing things under control, or creating trust) and often occurs in situations of real human distress.

It is not uncommon that rescuers have a personal or family history in which someone vulnerable needed to be saved from a harmful situation or perhaps (even if only imagined) could have been saved from death. There may have been a sick parent or sibling, or someone being mistreated in some way. A nurturing trait may have begun to develop which was subsequently carried into adult life in the form of rescuing.

Alternatively, a rescuer may be nursing their own trauma or negative experiences of the past or present. Stepping in to save others may be a projection of some aspect of one's own experience and an attempt at saving oneself from past or present pain; it may represent symbolic self-healing, despite the problem of focus being someone else's. Either of these background reasons for rescuing may help explain the passion and persistence with which some rescuers throw themselves so fully into 'saving' others. It may also explain their intuitive ability to spot another person's vulnerability, that they are in trouble, or somewhat isolated in their emotional pain.

Perhaps all of us have stepped over the line into the territory of rescuing. Because it is a common error, it is important, especially for those of us working in the field of human services, to cultivate self-insight and self-awareness. Quite apart from the unhelpful nature of rescuing for the rescued, the rescuer does themselves no favours and can be negatively affected in a range of ways.

> Quite apart from the unhelpful nature of rescuing for the rescued, the rescuer does themselves no favours and can be negatively affected in a range of ways.

Avoiding this behaviour to the extent possible, is a vital principal of self-care and self-preservation. We cannot competently and compassionately help and support others unless we also pay attention to ourselves and our own needs. As was noted in the previous chapter, these things stand or fall together and constitute a single moral imperative of human service.

Profile of a rescuer 	Bad effects experienced by a rescuer
Treats the needs of others as more important than their own	Self-neglect. May hardly have a life of their own. May deprive their own family of their emotional presence. May take less and less responsibility for self-care, personal and interpersonal issues
Over-investment of energy in other's need for change or adaptation	Emotional depletion and fatigue
Persists in helping others even when it has been communicated that their help is no longer needed	Potential rejection and feelings of hurt and discouragement
Doesn't ask how others want to be helped, but presumes to know and rescue anyway	Should this not be appreciated, self-doubt can set in, with a global questioning of self-competence
Want other people to need them and appreciate them. Unwittingly seek to meet their own need of affirmation and acceptance	If this doesn't appear to occur, can feel rejected, angry, unappreciated, deflated, and may exhibit a 'martyr complex'. May never feel content except on the treadmill of helping others
When others ask for assistance and there is not time to provide it, guilt may result	Feeling stressed and a failure for not being able to respond; exhausted by the weight of unmet need
Struggle to focus or to complete work because rescuing overstretches personal capacity	Become drawn into the harmful 'slippery slope' of 'burn out'
Doesn't ask for feedback unless positive feedback can be assured	Self becomes so overprotected that criticism is acutely painful and threatening, and inflexibility and rigidity of attitude, thinking and behaviour can set in
Reluctant to refer on to another professional or co-worker, for fear of admitting they can't help or are not accepted by a client/patient, or for fear of feeling powerless and worthless	A background sense of guilt or doubt may emerge, due to knowing at some level that the best interests of the person being 'helped' have become supplanted by self-interest, which if ignored can become generally corrosive of self-respect and self-image
May consume alcohol or smoke cigarettes with little thought for their effects, due to needing to self-medicate stress, and because it becomes easy to justify given how important the focus on others has become; is construed and justified sub-consciously as an acceptable part of self-sacrifice	Unknowing or ignored dependence on alcohol and/or cigarettes, with the risk that carries

Setting Boundaries for Self-preservation

In the first chapter the idea that you must matter was repeatedly emphasised because of the moral contradictoriness of ignoring our own wellbeing. How can we continue to help others competently and compassionately if we are over-tired, or mentally and emotionally depleted? Setting boundaries and correctly framing the way we approach working with others in a helping capacity is essential to self-care and self-preservation. It can also contribute to us achieving the most economical and optimal use of our personal capacity in a way that is sustainable over the long haul. The following components of boundary setting are worthy of reflection:

When elements of friendship seep into a 'helping relationship'

Even if you've had training that clearly defined the scope of a *helping relationship*, it may be useful to review some aspects of this again to observe ways in which 'slippage' can occur with potential for you to find yourself in a place where self-care may be compromised.

A helping relationship incorporates concern, compassion, attentiveness, reliability, commitment, warmth, and authentic human encounters and exchanges. It affords the person being helped the opportunity for self-disclosure, being known, affirmed, valued, and respected. These are all vitally important elements in an effective helping relationship, and reflect *common factors* that have been identified as contributing substantially to positive outcomes in counselling and psychotherapy, much more than the potential of techniques or therapy model based strategies.

A helping relationship requires that it is usually time limited, contractual, and subject to termination. The helping relationship occurs in a work space or the client/patient's space, not our own personal space. It is goal or outcome oriented, has allotted tasks and responsibilities, and incorporates a process of progressive review and monitoring. In this relationship, we avoid having a greater investment of energy than is exhibited by the person being helped (with some exceptions such as, medical and nursing care).

> A helping relationship requires that it is usually time limited, contractual, and subject to termination.

It is a relationship that is usually documented, accountable, and confidential. It also has legal implications including a duty of care, safe storage of documentation, disclosure requirements, and the possibility of case-notes or clinical records being subpoenaed.

In contrast, a friendship tends to be open-ended – without formal boundaries on things like time, responsibility, what is personal and what is not, and how it impinges on personal energy and privacy. In common with the helping relationship, it incorporates concern, compassion, attentiveness, reliability, commitment, warmth, and authentic human encounters and exchanges. It affords a person the opportunity for self-disclosure, being known, affirmed, valued, and respected.

The characteristics that both friendship and the helping relationship have in common are essential to effective helping, but as well, its greatest potential vulnerability. Clients and patients usually understand without any coaching, that exchanges of a sexual nature with their human service worker are prohibited ethically; but without knowledge of the nature of a helping relationship, they have no way of differentiating what they are most familiar with, friendship, from a helping relationship. Even if the boundaries, limitations, and responsibilities of a helping relationship are spelt out at the beginning of the relationship, these may be poorly comprehended or quickly forgotten – especially by a client or patient experiencing distress.

Self-care in this setting means watching out for subtle signs of boundaries either not being understood by clients or patients, or being shifted by them. This usually occurs with little consciousness on their part, and may creep up on you unexpectedly, resulting in an awkward situation which may not be remediable without distress for both of you. The ways in which this slippage commonly occurs, which you'll need to watch out for and 'nip in the bud' may include:

- Allowing length or number of visits or sessions to be extended without clear purpose, comment or correction
- Growing interpersonal familiarity that extends beyond constructiveness and has an emotionally reciprocal quality

- Communication to your phone or email by a client/patient, which may have a formal and practical component yet which exhibits a familiarity not permitted or encouraged in visits or sessions
- Client/patient giving you gifts
- Subtle physical contact by a client/patient that feels intuitively unsettling
- Growing client/patient inquisitiveness about your personal or family life
- Client/patient wanting to stay in touch after their discharge from your service
- Client/patient misreading of self-disclosure you may have used to aid a counselling or psychotherapeutic process. For them this may have suggested an invitation to familiarity more characteristic of friendship
- Client/patient (in a rural or small town setting) who knows you outside of your work role, or members of your familial or social circle, may expect to have privileged access to you, or liberty of greater familiarity than a helping relationship

Problem ownership

To engage fully with another person and their experience of their problems is fundamental to human service and has the potential to make a positive and lasting difference to their life. The inherent hazard in this kind of engagement, is not being conscious of or able to 'switch off' or disengage when you need to, either to move on to the next person you are helping or to go home to your personal life and family. This doesn't mean that you cease to care, it just means that you need to be able to acknowledge other people's ownership of their problems and experience.

You may have heard it said: 'the poor will always be with us'? Though we may agree, this isn't the way the world should be, it is the way the world actually is. There is only so much you can do personally; there are many people and situations you have no power to help or change. Accepting these facts are a key not only to self-care and self-preservation, but are essential to you maintaining your capacity for compassion and human service, with long lived continuity rather than just

> There is only so much you can do personally; there are many people and situations you have no power to help or change.

bursting on the scene like a bright comet, only to burn itself out and disappear from view.

Often, people who become cynically indifferent to other people's plight, or must withdraw exhausted from human service work, are those who have not practised problem ownership. If our concern for a person extends to feeling a sense of ownership or personal responsibility for their problems or their experience, we are breaching appropriate boundaries. Should we assume this stance in helping a number of people, we stand the risk of becoming overwhelmed and ineffectual.

We engage with people to help them with *their* problems. On returning to our own personal space, or needing to engage with someone else or another task, we need to be able to leave people with *their* 'property'- their experience and their problems. We don't cease to care about them, that continues, but we do not take ownership of their experience or problems, we must disengage from both. Though caring yet disengaging may sound too subtle, with some practice, it is an internal mechanism we can create. We can do this by cultivating self-awareness and through some simple self-dialogue: 'I care about this person, but I must now disengage and turn my attention to someone else', or, 'my own personal life'.

> On returning to our own personal space, or needing to engage with someone else or another task, we need to be able to leave people with their 'property'- their experience and their problems.

Practising problem ownership in working with people we care about, means taking steps to value ourselves and to preserve a capacity for ongoing energetic and effective service to others.

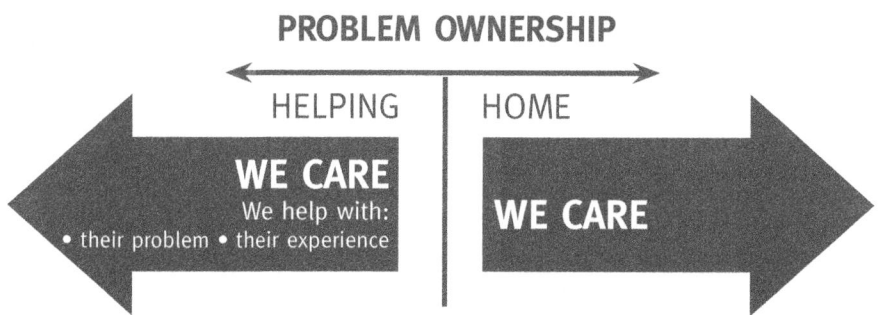

PROBLEM OWNERSHIP

HELPING | HOME

WE CARE
We help with:
• their problem • their experience

WE CARE

Managing Emotional Involvement

Exposure to other people's emotion and distress is an inevitable part of being with, supporting and helping other people humanly. Such exposure can not only affect us in the moment, but can also *effect* changes in the way we deal with and manage our own experience, and not always in a positive way. Experiencing other's emotion can powerfully modify and re-route neural pathways in our brain; it can affect how we subsequently think, feel, and behave. This shouldn't be a discouragement to us engaging with people humanly, rather it suggests that we need to learn how to manage our experience of others emotion and distress, so it doesn't impair our own emotional wellbeing or our capacity for continuing to carry out our helping role effectively.

Some nurses trained under 'old school nursing' models were taught strictly, 'not to get involved' and to practice personal and emotional detachment in caring for patients. This behavioural convention has resulted in patients sometimes encountering callous and miserable nursing 'care' at a time of acute vulnerability and personal isolation. It has also meant nurses themselves struggling with much internal confusion having to somehow reconcile being caring with being detached and un-emotional.

This has been a misguided and unnecessary dichotomy. Clearly, to engage with others humanly and compassionately is a fundamental principle of human service, as is learning how to manage the inevitable personal effects of doing so. We have already explored the idea of problem ownership. Another effective way of putting things in perspective is talking to a colleague about your experience of caring for or helping someone else. This engages the region of your brain (the left prefrontal cortex) responsible for functions such as reasoning and problem solving in order to counter balance the sometimes overpowering feelings generated from those parts of your brain referred to as the limbic system.

> Clearly, to engage with others humanly and compassionately is a fundamental principle of human service, as is learning how to manage the inevitable personal effects of doing so.

There is another way of regulating the effects of others emotions and distress in your experience, and that is to learn how to *manage your emotional involvement*. Similar to what was said of problem ownership, this involves creating an internal mechanism, cultivating emotion self-awareness and self-monitoring, and an internal dialogue (in your mind or, 'under your breath') while you are working with and in the presence of a client or patient. This might be something like: 'I'm feeling this more than I want to or that might be good for me; I need to pull back a little'. All of us have this capacity, termed *metacognition*; the ability to observe and think about our own thoughts and emotions.

With practice, it is possible to monitor your emotional involvement so that you can decide to pull back from or regulate down your emotional response to a client's or patient's emotion or distress, not to the extent of detachment (potentially leaving the person feeling isolated), but for you to avoid being unduly affected. The idea here is to avoid detachment or over-involvement (both of which are undesirable) and to 'lean into' another's emotion state or distress sufficient for effective rapport and for continuity of caring, and, so that you can also return to an emotional and mental posture that enables you to move on to the next client or patient or your personal time without personal ill-effects.

> With practice, it is possible to monitor your emotional involvement so that you can decide to pull back from or regulate down your emotional response to a client's or patient's emotion or distress.

MINDFULLY MONITORING OUR EMOTIONAL INVOLVEMENT

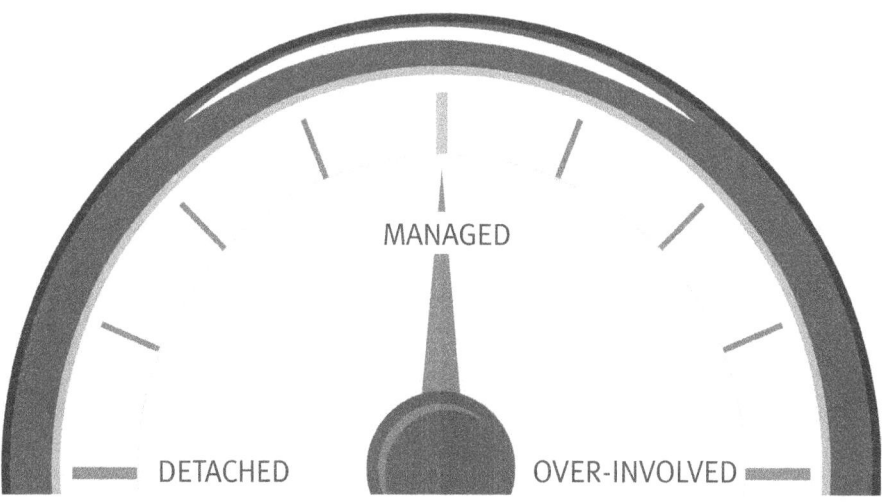

MANAGED EMOTIONAL INVOLVEMENT

Over-involved – we may become psychologically depleted

Detached – we may feel 'safe' but will likely be ineffectual and a person may be left feeling isolated

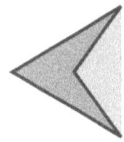
Being self-aware and 'leaning into' another's experience – permits managed emotional involvement and withdrawal

Saying 'no' to the Tyranny of Devices

One of the most insidious threats to self-care and self-preservation is the unchallenged and habit forming use of technology, our everyday devices. Perhaps the most notable of these is the smart phone. Once upon a time (yes, this is going to be something from the distant past), if you were expecting an urgent call you would let the people around you know so that it didn't appear rude when you asked to be excused when the call came through. Or, if you were at dinner and someone answered the telephone and the call happened to be for you, unless of an urgent nature, it would not be allowed priority over your dinner engagement and you would give instruction for the caller to be told that you will call them back once your dinner was over or most likely the following day.

It is now commonplace to respond to phone calls, text messages and even emails in the middle of dinner, a staff meeting, a conference, training event, or even a personal conversation. Increasingly now, when couples dine out they spend the whole time (in-between shovelling in mouthfuls of food which they hardly even notice the taste of) texting or emailing on their phones and making no more eye contact with each other than with the service staff. Well, that is a whole topic for another time, as is the way Facebook has become such a social 'necessity' eating up many hours each day of people's recreation and work time. But you'd be an exception to the rule if you said you haven't noticed these things, or that you haven't had at least a brush with the addictive power of gadget communication instantaneity.

Let's assume you have cultivated some maturity in learning to say 'no' to unreasonable demands on your time, mental and emotional capacities in a variety of ways – which is an essential principle of self-care. What about when it comes to emails, text messages and mobile calls? The almost unquestioned and unregulated obligation associated with these communications has crept up on us and established itself in our lives often in direct violation of personal disciplines and choices formerly established to ensure self-care and to avoid overload.

When an email arrives, how obligated do you feel to respond with greater haste than if a letter arrived by mail? When a call or text message arrives on your mobile phone, what priority of response do you give it? On a busy work day, you may be quite disciplined about not being interrupted, why is it then that you feel obliged to take a call on your mobile phone unless it is of considerable importance or urgency? Why indeed do you permit others to interrupt and intrude on your busy day without invitation?

With modern devices, there are all kinds of ways of regulating the traffic of communications, so there is little excuse not to unless *you* choose not to. There isn't space here to go into the psychological complexities of group inclusion behaviour, constructs of social obligation, addiction and reward mechanisms of the brain, obsessive-compulsive tendencies, or the persuasiveness of gadgets in shaping our reflexive and behavioural responses. Suffice to say, communication intrusions and collusive interaction with them poses a major potential threat to the manageability of not just daily work flow and routines, but that of mental health and wellbeing.

> With modern devices, there are all kinds of ways of regulating the traffic of communications, so there is little excuse not to unless you choose not to.

If you don't want any longer to allow 'the tail to wag the dog', because you take self-care seriously, here are some simple suggestions for you to consider:

- Switch off automatic email and text notifications on your computer and mobile device

- Turn off your mobile device or activate mute when you are committed to a social engagement, personal or family time, a meeting, or a piece of work that requires uninterrupted concentration
- Have set times for answering emails each day, so that you aren't tempted to keep checking them as they come in or throughout the day
- Take the time to unsubscribe to unwanted or unnecessary email ads (they'll come again otherwise). If you need or want something of the kind they mention, star the email, so you can find it again if you choose to.
- Sit down and make a calculation about how much time is taken up with Facebook activity that isn't really of benefit to you
- Take a count of the number of times you check your phone each day to gauge how much of your attention it takes up (and perhaps how much of your employer's time)

Work and Play: Achieving a Sustainable Ratio

Doubtless you've heard a health or wellness commentator extolling the virtues of a 'work/life balance'? The phrase is so often mentioned, it has become rather trite and mentally dismissible like many other popular catchphrases. Another reason it is easy to ignore is because of what it implies (even if it's not meant to), some sort of 50/50 balance of work and non-work, the latter being occupied with recreation, exercise, perhaps meditation, and the pursuit of personal interests. Of course, such an idea is a nonsense for the vast majority of people who work full time and could not possibly contemplate such a luxury. Having said that, there is of course considerable merit for self-preservation and self-care in achieving a better ratio and relationship of work versus non-work activities.

Our work and our occupational projects may well be very important and meaningful for us, they may be what provides us with mental stimulation, social interaction and inclusion, and a daily sense of purpose that is fundamental to our lives. And this isn't only true for men, increasingly it is true for many women as well. And, whilst we don't discount the value of other important elements of life - like exercise, relaxation, relationships and family, and our mental and emotional development, we may not be taking them seriously enough. Fatigue, a high level of stress, diminishing quality of relationships, a decline in creative output, and depression, may all be signs that we have yet to genuinely address the work/play issue.

If we become too absorbed in our work or projects, vitally important though they may be, we can end up functioning out on the periphery of ourselves - out of touch with the part of us that is most perceptive and capable of deep feeling, pleasure, and simple reflective satisfaction. We can become like tourists in life: taking snap shots of things without fully exploring, comprehending or experiencing them. We can become disconnected from our capacity for reading important emotional cues and signals in our relationships. Desensitised to the needs and feelings of others, we can become alienated from the very ones all our hard work may be meant to ultimately benefit.

The critical test is to step back from our work and projects and see how long we can bear it; to see if we have the capacity to relax, relieve stress, and focus on other priorities - especially relationships, without undue agitation, and with genuine and patient interest. If we can't, it's a clear indication that we may need to rethink and readjust our priorities.

Though what constitutes a sustainable ratio will be different for each of us, working out what may need to be given more attention, and in what way, will invariably require thoughtful, reflective, and genuinely honest assessment.

One suggestion is to draw a bar graph, using the different height of several bars to indicate important areas of your life, and the current relative attention they receive. This can help put things into perspective, and indicate what needs attention and how much. The bars don't necessarily have to achieve an equal height. Rather, they need to achieve a relative height that fits with what you honestly and realistically consider to be the kind of ratio that is healthy for you, and is sustainable over time. Use a diary or calendar to indicate dates for periodic review.

The thing to remember about the ratio of these elements is that it isn't a constant; it will change as things change in life - so it needs to be periodically reassessed. But it's well worth the effort and, far from detracting from your work and projects, can breathe new life into them.

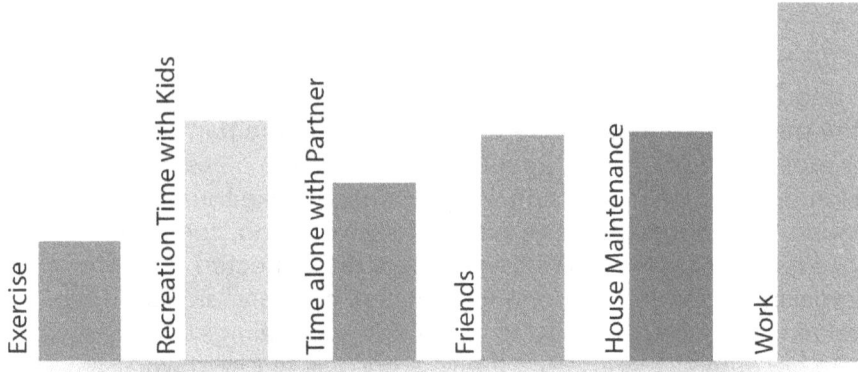

Taking Care of Yourself After a Critical Incident

There is potential to experience a critical incident in any form of human service work, so having a basic framework for knowing how to take care of yourself has considerable merit. First let's begin with a basic definition: *A critical incident is any event (or series of events) that is sudden (though not necessarily dramatic), threatening, significantly stressful, overwhelming, or that causes you to question your assumptions, beliefs, values, personal adequacy, or competence. Critical incidents may involve conflict, hostility, aggression, criticism, threat, death, or injury, and may be brief or protracted. An incident may leave you in shock, feeling emotionally numb, shaken, highly anxious, fearful, or seriously questioning yourself.*

Exposure to a critical incident can have more than just an initial effect, it can undermine your confidence, make you hyperalert, cause ongoing distress, anxiety, restlessness, mood disturbance, lethargy, sleep disturbance, a decline in work performance or in your overall sense of wellbeing.

There are several generally accepted strategies for managing the personal effects of a critical incident in a workplace, which also apply (with some adaptation) to contexts outside of work:

Taking time out to achieve a sense of calm

Because critical incidents can trigger a range of physiological and psychological effects, such as high blood pressure and anxiety, it is best if possible, to take some time away from work duties to allow for some calm, and engaging in a *demobilisation* process. Such a process is usually best facilitated or assisted by someone else who is unaffected or less affected by the incident. The elements of this process will include:

- bringing together those affected by the incident
- establishing and summarising the facts of the incident
- fielding any questions or concerns
- providing immediate support or care – which may also include seeking out an appropriate health professional to provide this
- formulating a basic plan of action to address any ongoing needs of individuals involved
- problem solve short-term arrangements to cover staff/worker responsibilities if an individual needs time away from their role
- ensure that everyone is aware of appropriate support providers should they be needed

You'll notice with this process that it doesn't put the focus on your emotions. The reason being, that to do so may tend to reinforce and anchor them unhelpfully, when what is needed is to activate your left prefrontal cortex in counterbalancing emotion and helping you attain perspective.

If you happen to be working alone, you may need to consider seeking out a colleague, peer, or friend to work you through relevant components of this process (which includes the additional ones following).

Proximate follow-up and review

This second phase of response (no later than the next working day or earlier if possible) is important as a way of monitoring your progress through the experience you have had, and for covering new questions, sharing your current experience, identifying any needs, and creating a future opportunity for a final debriefing. It may involve:

- talking about and reviewing the event
- discussing any questions or concerns
- clarifying any needs
- requesting any information needed for support
- arranging a final debriefing session

This phase of response is all about helping you commence some progress in achieving a new equilibrium - a workable balance that sees things like your sleep, physiological arousal mechanisms, thought activity, and emotion sensitivity return to a more even and sustainable place.

Debriefing

Debriefing is best arranged to occur within a week of the critical incident; which will have allowed you some time to have taken in and processed your experience further. It is not counselling, but a more basic process of reinforcing a perspective of the incident that is clear, sustainable, and helpful to your full recovery. This phase of response may include:

- again, being helped to review the sequence of events surrounding the critical incident
- observing causes and consequences
- checking in with your current experience - including identifying any memories triggered by the event
- normalising your experience (if possible in relation to other people's)
- again, identifying any needs you have that might benefit from follow up with an appropriate health professional

Monitoring for any need of follow-up support

Stress responses to critical incidents can linger and even develop over time. Further sessions after the debriefing session may be needed just for reinforcement and maintenance, or to focus on new and emerging personal experience and any recent issues relating to the incident that may need consideration and resolution. It is important to acknowledge that no single experience of an event happens in isolation, it may reactivate painful historic memories, trigger defenses, uncover stored or delayed grief, or may temporarily exacerbate vulnerabilities of mood or anxiety. It may decompensate you so that you handle stress poorly. This of course may all be manageable, but if not, do yourself a favour and talk to an appropriate health professional. Even a single session might make all the difference.

Bad Experiences Can Rub Off on You

For human service workers, there are emotional and psychological risks associated with providing services to vulnerable individuals. Nearly all of us during our lifetime are exposed to at least one traumatic event, however, working in the field of human services we are more prone to this type of exposure.

> Human service workers who assist traumatised people can develop symptoms of trauma and experience trauma themselves.

Whilst helping people in difficulty can certainly provide us with meaning and occupational satisfaction, we may face situations of human powerlessness, distress and suffering that can lead to our own physical and psychological health problems. Human service workers who assist traumatised people can develop symptoms of trauma and experience trauma themselves. For those who work regularly with people in crisis and distress, such exposure must be a major consideration in what defines the measures needed for their adequate self-care.

It is important for us to understand the nature of this landscape of hazards, and the terminology that has developed to describe it. Some of the terms used to describe this landscape are: Compassion Fatigue, Burnout, Vicarious Traumatisation, and Secondary Traumatic Stress. Each of these will be defined and briefly discussed.

There is value at this point in again reiterating the principle of altruism as a moral imperative of human service that includes both our wellbeing and that of those whom we help. There is now a range of evidence to suggest that when human service workers exercise compassion and due regard for themselves, and not just toward their clients, they are much more immune to compassion fatigue and burnout, and create a buffer against the effects of vicarious and secondary psychological trauma.

Compassion Fatigue

This is a cumulative chronic experience describing:
- emotional and physical fatigue
- mental tiredness and dullness

Compassion Fatigue occurs due to the chronic and frequent use of empathy in working with people who are suffering in some way, particularly where they make little progress or remain in a state or circumstances of powerlessness. These features of difficulty are all too often combined with day-to-day bureaucratic hurdles, workplace stress (which is contagious), and constantly trying to complete administrative work in competition with direct service delivery.

> Compassion Fatigue occurs due to the chronic and frequent use of empathy in working with people who are suffering in some way.

Self-care

Some of the best preventatives that offer a buffer against the effects of Compassion Fatigue include:
- maintaining physical fitness and health
- good balanced nutrition
- adequate sleep
- recreational activity
- positive forms of self-expression (like creative activities, cooking, gardening)

- mindfulness and meditative practices and yoga
- philanthropic and social volunteering activities that are personally revitalising
- social and emotional support
- negotiating a realistic and manageable workload and work routines and responsibilities (and making a time for periodic review)
- utilising lunch and refreshment breaks in a self-caring way (relaxing, walking, engaging in pleasurable activity, going to another room (other than your workspace) to drink or eat
- seeking out support from colleagues (who may also be interested in reciprocating)
- the other measures mentioned in this book

Counselling or Psychotherapy

If you are already experiencing or beginning to experience the effects of Compassion Fatigue, you may benefit considerably from counselling or psychotherapy with a practitioner experienced in working with this difficulty.

Burnout

This is a cumulative chronic experience characterised by:
- feeling emotionally depleted and exhausted
- feeling depersonalised or not feeling yourself in a connected way (maybe feeling a bit like an impersonal machine going through the motions), experiencing a dulled connection with other people and your environment, and a loss of emotional responsiveness
- a reduced sense of personal accomplishment

Burnout can happen if the emotional expectations that are part of your role, such as needing to repress or display emotions routinely, and frequently use empathy, are too burdensome or are not sufficiently counterbalanced by adequate self-care. Other factors contributing to burnout may include: conflict with co-workers,

> Burnout can happen if the emotional expectations that are part of your role, such as needing to repress or display emotions routinely, and frequently use empathy, are too burdensome or are not sufficiently counterbalanced by adequate self-care.

your individual coping style and personality, and the demands of interacting with and understanding clients or patients.

Some of the tell-tale signs of burnout creeping up on you may include: you've needed to take days off work to revive, getting behind with work tasks such as administration and case-notes, and not keeping up with tasks important to clients or patients. You may also find yourself becoming fatigued, distracted, sleeping poorly, feeling stressed nearly all the time, irritable, and increasingly pessimistic.

Self-care

Some of the best preventatives that offer a buffer against the effects of Burnout include:
- maintaining physical fitness and health
- good balanced nutrition
- adequate sleep
- recreational activity
- positive forms of self-expression (like creative activities, cooking, gardening)
- mindfulness and meditative practices and yoga
- philanthropic and social volunteering activities that are personally revitalising
- social and emotional support
- negotiating a realistic and manageable workload and work routines and responsibilities (and making a time for periodic review)
- utilising lunch and refreshment breaks in a self-caring way (relaxing, walking, engaging in pleasurable activity, going to another room (other that workspace) to drink or eat
- seeking out support from colleagues (who may also be interested in reciprocating)
- taking the time to deal with and work through workplace difficulties (such as interpersonal conflict)
- the other measures mentioned in this book

Counselling or Psychotherapy

If you are already experiencing or beginning to experience the effects of Burnout, you may benefit considerably from counselling or psychotherapy with a practitioner experienced in working with this difficulty.

Vicarious Traumatisation

This is an experience that is more immediate in onset than Compassion Fatigue or Burnout. Some of its characteristics include:
- alterations in your sense of self
- changes in your world views about key issues such as safety, trust, and control
- social withdrawal
- onset of cynicism and/or pessimism
- diminished emotional sensitivity and reactivity
- altered sense of previously held spiritual beliefs
- fatigue and change in sleep pattern
- feeling less comfortable in your own company

Vicarious traumatisation is a process of personal (cognitive) change that occurs due to exposure to client's or patient's traumatic experiences. If your work involves listening to other's memories and descriptions of very painful or frightening traumatic experiences, you are in a role that could make you vulnerable to this condition.

> If your work involves listening to other's memories and descriptions of very painful or frightening traumatic experiences, you are in a role that could make you vulnerable to this condition.

Self-care

Your vulnerability to this condition may be heightened if you have a pre-existing history of anxiety or mood disturbance difficulties, or a personal history of psychological trauma. Put simply, there may be something in your past that predisposes you to this experience.

Managing the potential risks of Vicarious Traumatisation may include:
- anticipating coping difficulties by being pro-active in selecting self-care strategies most suited to your role and your known vulnerabilities. Being organised ahead of time is vital
- ensuring that you have in place and keep in place counterbalancing self-care activities like: rest, recreation, exercise, yoga, social contact and interaction with friends and family
- mindfulness and meditation practices
- counselling: you might arrange a periodic visit to a suitable counsellor with whom you can discuss your experiences, to

process them in a systematic way (something you can't do with family or friends). This can enable you to keep your mind and emotions in check, your experience in perspective, and a positive and balanced outlook (avoiding cynicism or pessimism room to develop)
- good balanced nutrition
- adequate sleep
- positive forms of self-expression (like creative activities, cooking, gardening)
- philanthropic and social volunteering activities that are personally revitalising
- the other measures mentioned in this book

Counselling or Psychotherapy

If you are already experiencing or beginning to experience the effects of Vicarious Traumatisation, you may benefit considerably from counselling or psychotherapy with a practitioner experienced in working with this difficulty.

Secondary Traumatic Stress

This is an experience that is more immediate in onset than Compassion Fatigue or Burnout. Its characteristics may include the full range of symptoms described as Post Traumatic Stress Disorder (PTSD), including:
- intrusive thoughts
- traumatic memories or nightmares associated with client/patient trauma,
- insomnia
- chronic irritability or angry outbursts
- fatigue
- general anxiety and mood disturbance
- difficulty concentrating
- avoidance of further client/patient situations with any hint of similar elements of the original traumatic client/patient event
- hypervigilant or startle reactions toward stimuli or reminders of the client's/patient's trauma

Secondary Traumatic Stress (STS) refers to emotional, cognitive, and behavioural effects of 'engaging' with a traumatic event experienced by a client/patient through knowing about the event experienced by them, and the stress resulting from helping or wanting to help them.

STS results from entering an empathic relationship with an individual suffering from a traumatic experience and bearing witness to the intensity and emotional content of their experience. The symptoms of STS mirror the symptoms of PTSD experienced by the primary victim of trauma.

> STS results from entering an empathic relationship with an individual suffering from a traumatic experience and bearing witness to the intensity and emotional content of their experience.

Self-care

Your vulnerability to this condition may be heightened if you have a pre-existing history of anxiety or mood disturbance difficulties, or a personal history of psychological trauma. Put simply, there may be something in your past that predisposes you to this experience.

Some of the best preventatives that offer a buffer against the effects of STS include:

- maintaining physical fitness and health
- good balanced nutrition
- adequate sleep
- recreational activity
- positive forms of self-expression (like creative activities, cooking, gardening)
- mindfulness and meditative practices and yoga
- philanthropic and social volunteering activities that are personally revitalising
- social and emotional support
- the other measures mentioned in this book

Counselling or Psychotherapy

If you are already experiencing or beginning to experience the effects of Secondary Traumatic Stress, you may benefit considerably from counselling or psychotherapy with a practitioner experienced in working with this difficulty.

Learning to Manage Stress

Everyone knows what it's like to experience stress. And most people would agree that it usually isn't very pleasant. Not surprisingly, our stress now supports a growth industry, which markets stress reduction workshops, massage, supplements, and all manner of online relaxation resources. But few people fully understand the nature of stress, its effects, and the significant difference in the way it is experienced by men and women, and how this is exhibited in behavior.

The 'stress response' has its origins in our primitive past - when our ancestors frequently faced dangerous predators or enemies. It provided quick bursts of energy, strength, and alertness, needed to stand and fight - or run away. Still 'wired' into our brains today, it involves a complex array of chemical reactions and changes in body function. Unfortunately, because the mundane aggravations of daily life can also activate the stress response, we experience the same surge of body chemicals and changes in body function, designed for much less frequent major threats. Stressed too frequently, or for prolonged periods, our bodies take a terrible pounding.

This biochemical onslaught can compromise our immune system, making us vulnerable to infection and disease - including cancer. Hormones unleashed by stress can damage the digestive tract and lungs; they can also weaken the heart, leading to stroke and heart disease. Prolonged stress can eat away at every body system like an internal predator. Though it can protect us, it can also turn on us.

> Prolonged stress can eat away at every body system like an internal predator. Though it can protect us, it can also turn on us.

Recent research indicates that some people are more prone to stress than others. Losing a parent, being traumatised, or in some other way being exposed to a high level of stress in childhood, may permanently rewire the brain's circuitry, making it much more difficult to deal with everyday stress in later life. But whatever our individual tolerance for stress, it can - and needs to be managed.

Unfortunately, amongst the first casualties of stress with men may be: communication, sensitivity, patience, empathy, and being sociable – and it's important to understand why.

Both men and women experience the stress response, or 'fight or flight' response, but then something surprisingly different happens. In women, a hormone call oxytocin is secreted which, in combination with and boosted by the female sex hormone estrogen, has not only a calming effect, but prompts them to be more empathic, nurturing and sociable. This has been termed the 'tend and befriend response'. In addition, women benefit from being emotionally and verbally expressive, and seeking empathy from others. Their ability to read others' emotional cues – such as facial cues, becomes enhanced.

In contrast, men not only experience the 'fight or flight' response, but they register higher levels of stress hormones (adrenaline and cortisol), which stay in their system longer. The male sex hormone testosterone inhibits oxytocin release under conditions of stress, which, along with stress hormones, promotes less social and more aggressive task-focused behaviours. Males become less sociable, have a diminished capacity for empathy, and have difficulty reading others' facial expressions – important for appreciating others' emotional experience. Under conditions of acute and chronic stress, males may tend to be more reactive, irritable, angry, argumentative, and less communicative and sensitive towards others.

The male response to stress may also help to explain why alcohol misuse, as a form of self-medication for the relief of stress, is a predominantly male behavior, one which is known to trigger or worsen mental health difficulties such as insomnia and depression. Men who drink alcohol immoderately (compared to abstinence) are also at much greater risk of suicide (some estimates suggest 90 times greater risk).

Again, in contrast to women, men characteristically benefit less from being verbally and emotionally expressive, and more from sharing tasks with other males and just being alongside them. For males, emotion and stress are often dispersed through action, physical activity, and practical tasks.

It can help in understanding these male/female differences under stress, if we consider our hunter/gatherer past. Imagine a community under threat from a marauding tribe: the men would naturally be at the forefront in fighting off the aggressors, and to do so they would need to be fueled by hormones and energy boosting adrenalin until the job was done. It might put them and the community at greater risk and result in defeat, if they were to view their aggressors with empathy, or to pay attention to anything other than aggressively pursuing the task at hand: defeating their enemies.

Women in these circumstances would also have needed the whole of body system activating effects of the 'fight or flight' response – at least at first, but then an enhanced sense of the need to affiliate with other women to protect offspring, and to provision their male protectors so that the whole community had the best chance of survival. It is interesting to note that in situations of disaster, community trauma, and adverse climatic events, these stress responses are still largely true to form and are our default settings.

> It is interesting to note that in situations of disaster, community trauma, and adverse climatic events, these stress responses are still largely true to form and are our default settings.

Even when men and women experience moderate degrees of stress, the characteristic male and female responses will often become evident. Of course, stress is still an individual experience, which varies from one individual to another, and there will also be exceptions to the rule when it comes to on-average male and female responses to stress. Notwithstanding this, the on-average stress response profiles still hold true.

Here are some strategies to consider and act on:
- Structured problem solving: tackling problems that give rise to stress in a thoughtful, step-by-step, constructive, and deliberate way. Writing things down on paper is best. This may also involve gaining the advice of others who can help in this process
- Daily exercise - especially before your evening meal. This can help burn off stress hormones in the bloodstream, and stimulate neurotransmitters in the brain responsible for modulating mood and emotion
- Limiting alcohol intake to a low risk level (alcohol interferes with sleep and depresses mood)
- Cutting out caffeine (caffeine acts as an unwanted stimulant and interferes with sleep; it can make stress worse)
- Slowing life down, and deliberately engaging in calming activities and recreation. Going about ordinary tasks more slowly and deliberately - *slowing physical motion* can be very effective
- Writing down what is most important to you - getting back in touch with your deepest values
- Finding a good relaxation technique (one that works and that is easy to practice), and using it several times a day
- Learning to control your thoughts. Disciplining yourself to think rationally about challenges and problems, and avoiding:

  - Catastrophising ('this is the worst thing that could happen to me')

  - Globalising ('everything has gone wrong; nothing will help')

  Both responses generate a lot of stress. If replaced by structured problem solving, an experience and/or problem can be cut down to size. Things that are in fact going well, and options previously not recognised, can be highlighted

- Learning about stress reduction techniques. One size doesn't fit all. Discovering techniques that work for you personally
- Developing the discipline and cycle of getting to bed at night and waking in the mornings at much the same time, and making sure you get plenty of sleep

Try this simple relaxation technique (diaphragm or 'belly breathing' as it is sometimes called):

- *Breathe in slowly and fully through your nose.* Make sure your shoulders are down and relaxed. In this exercise, your stomach should expand, but your chest should rise very little. So, if you want, you can place one hand on your stomach and the other on your chest so you can feel how you are breathing.
- *Exhale slowly through your mouth.* As you breathe air out, purse your lips slightly, but with your tongue and jaw relaxed. You may hear a soft 'whooshing' sound as you exhale. That's good, listen for that sound every time you practice and learn to value it as the sound of relaxation.
- *Repeat this breathing exercise for several minutes.* Make your outgoing breath as long and smooth as you can. The outgoing breath is the key to relaxation so give it your full attention and practice breathing out in a long slow controlled way and you will quickly feel the benefit.

All the above suggestions can be matched with resources readily available and downloadable from the internet. Here are some website addresses:
http://www.studygs.net/stress.htm
http://www.humanstress.ca/
http://www.webmd.com/ (search Stress)

Why Self-medication is a Poor Substitute for Self-care

The track record of human service workplaces as promoters of staff health and wellbeing is not always what it should be. Staff resorting to self-medication is not an uncommon response. Contrary to the *human wellbeing promoting value stance* of some human service organisations, such environments exhibit: little monitoring and management of work related stress, dealing poorly with or turning a blind eye to workplace conflict, not ensuring that staff have health preserving workloads and proper support, and a lack of initiative in encouraging and creating conditions conducive to staff generally taking care of themselves.

If you work in such an environment, there may be scope for you to challenge the prevailing culture and the disconnect between values and behaviour. If that's too likely to get you into 'deep water', or if you can't creatively manoeuvre around workplace 'health hazards', you may need to begin reflecting on the suitability of your employment. If you happen to be self-employed, you as your own employer have little excuse but to ensure conditions conducive to proper self-care!

Discussion of *self-medication* or *self-medicating recreation* involves some subtleties that require explanation. To begin with, there is an insidious susceptibility hidden beneath the surface of the human service psyche, which subtly justifies the use of alcohol and substances as an acceptable respite from self-sacrifice, or as a much-deserved reward for subjecting oneself to the stress and rigours of 'altruism'.

> There is an insidious susceptibility hidden beneath the surface of the human service psyche, which subtly justifies the use of alcohol and substances as an acceptable respite from self-sacrifice, or as a much-deserved reward for subjecting oneself to the stress and rigours of 'altruism'.

Another factor may also be at play here. We know for example that some people who smoke cigarettes, and who appear most impervious to their doctor's advice and very graphic media health warnings, have little sense of future or of present behavioural consequences reaching into the future; they live very much for the moment. Because potential consequences of smoking are not perceived as immediately significant, for such people they simply don't register as a risk to be taken seriously.

This *living for today* or limited *present time* mindset, can encourage sensation seeking, risk-taking hedonism, and a measure of fatalism – common behaviours amongst people in high stress occupations. Stress can make us feel like we are subject to influences beyond our control. For example, being subject to a constant and almost overwhelming stream of distressed clients can quickly encapsulate us in a limited present time experience and mindset. This is often tolerated and justified by a *self-exclusive* notion of altruism, self-sacrifice, and *human service*. In these circumstances, all that *is*, consists of a pervasive sense of stress and unrelenting client problems. Living for today, with little experienced sense of future (except that it might be more of the same) may give license to some measure of unconstraint, sensation-seeking, and sublimation of experience of an immediate kind. It may subtly justify self-medication or self-medicating recreation, contrary to and in place of self-care.

The fact is we generally have a lot more control over the pace and volume of the work we do than we might prefer to admit. An audit of our own potential motives for *drivenness* may be just as important as examining what others expect of us or of our role. And we certainly have choices about whether we manage our stress adaptively or maladaptively. In our line of work, we also have a responsibility for modelling appropriate choices and behaviours to our clients/patients. This in turn leads back to our definition of altruism which must include us giving due consideration to our own self-care and nurture. As already stated, care of others and care of self, stand or fall together, and comprise a single moral imperative of human service.

> An audit of our own potential motives for drivenness may be just as important as examining what others expect of us or of our role.

The most common forms of self-medication or self-medicating recreation used as a substitute for self-care involve: alcohol, nicotine, and caffeine. The use of any of these *psycho-active* substances or recreational drugs are self-defeating for purposes of managing elements of our workplace experience. We'll examine some facts about each of these, and why their use in this way is contrary to self-care. Historical and contemporary influences determining the human use of psycho-active agents are complex, and humans appear to have had a co-evolutionary relationship with them since time immemorial. However, with modern science and the human potential for longevity hitherto unimaginable to our ancestors, we have opportunity and good reason to consider the potential health implications of their use.

Alcohol

Alcohol use is a widely-accepted part of Australian culture, and alcohol is one of the most commonly used mood-changing recreational drugs. Based on self-reported data from the 2011-12 Australian Health Survey (AHS), 1 in 5 people aged 18 and over (20%) consume more than 2 standard drinks per day on average, exceeding the lifetime alcohol risk guidelines. The misuse of alcohol is one of the chief causes of preventable death in Australia, it is significantly implicated in social and domestic violence, and has a variety of negative effects on mental health.

Alcohol is a central nervous system depressant and not a stimulant as popularly believed. It slows the activity of the central nervous system, affecting concentration and coordination, and slowing the response time to unexpected situations. It has a variety of effects which vary for each individual. In some people, it appears to give rise to aggression. In others, it has the effect of causing them to be amorous, tearful, or perhaps talkative. Even moderate inebriation tends to induce disinhibition, more intense moods, and impaired judgement – which may mean that people react uncharacteristically or get involved in situations in which they wouldn't normally become involved (such as verbal and physical conflict and disinhibited sexual activity).

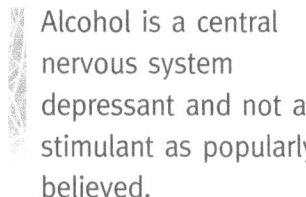

Alcohol is a central nervous system depressant and not a stimulant as popularly believed.

While alcohol in small doses may produce relaxation, a lowering of inhibitions, feelings of confidence, and more 'outgoingness', in larger quantities it can have a significant negative impact on mental and physical health.

Alcohol is commonly used as a form of self-medication, to help with sleep, and to dampen stress and anxiety. Many people who suffer insomnia use alcohol as an aid to sleep. And though it is effective in inducing sleep, it impairs sleep by causing multiple awakenings during the second half of the sleep period, and causes loss of overall sleep time, and daytime drowsiness. Sleep impairment can occur even when alcohol is consumed in the afternoon. Sleep impairment can also cause depression.

Research has now clearly revealed a cause and effect relationship between alcohol abuse and dependence and major depression. Clearly, alcohol not only potentially makes depression worse, it can cause depression.

As for stress and anxiety, though alcohol can temporarily dampen these, both are made worse through immoderate alcohol consumption. Other negative effects include difficulties of concentration and memory, sexual dysfunction, and a variety of cancers. Worryingly, alcohol intoxication also increases suicide risk by up to 90 times in susceptible individuals.

Interestingly, data from the Center for Disease Control and Prevention in the US suggest that most health care providers don't talk about alcohol, even with patients who drink to excess significantly endangering their health. Only one in six adults - and only one in four binge drinkers - say a health professional has ever discussed alcohol use with them. Even among adults who binge drink 10 or more times a month, only one in three have ever had a health professional talk with them about alcohol use.

As for stress and anxiety, though alcohol can temporarily dampen these, both are made worse through immoderate alcohol consumption.

Let's indulge in some speculation here and assume this pattern of not broaching the issue of alcohol consumption with patients or clients is much the same in Australia. Could it be that some health and human service professionals don't raise the issue, because at some level they feel uncomfortable about questioning immoderate consumption because it's a behaviour they themselves sometimes engage in? Is there any truth in it for you?

While there is no safe level of drinking, only low risk drinking, the National Health and Medical Research Council has developed a set of guidelines to help people make choices about how much they drink and the potential risks to their health.

For healthy men and women, drinking no more than 2 standard drinks on any day reduces the lifetime risk of harm from an alcohol-related disease or injury.

Some common questions about alcohol

1. Does drinking affect male sexual performance?

Yes. Immoderate drinking can cause sexual dysfunction. Most men are aware of the link between alcohol and erectile problems.

2. Is alcohol fattening?

Yes. Alcohol is high in calories and contains few nutrients or vitamins. Drinking beer or any other alcoholic drink adds calories to a person's diet, which can result in them gaining weight and which can lead to obesity.

3. Can a person save up their drinks for one good session?

No. Drinking more than 4 standard drinks on a single occasion more than doubles the relative risk of experiencing an injury in the following 6 hours. Increased health and mental health risks also ensue with this pattern of drinking.

4. Can a person drink when on medication?

Mixing alcohol with medications (either over-the-counter or prescription) can have unexpected and even dangerous effects. Alcohol may also affect how well the medication works. It is important to read the packaging and consumer medicines information with all medications to see if alcohol is mentioned.

5. Can alcohol help sleep?

No. Though alcohol may help a person to feel tired and to go to sleep, it usually causes disrupted and poor quality sleep.

6. How does alcohol affect mental health difficulties?

The relationship between alcohol and mental health difficulties is complex. As a general rule, they do not mix well. Alcohol can interfere with the effectiveness of many medications and can be dangerous when taken in combination with others.

7. Is a person at risk of developing an alcohol-related problem if their family has a history of alcohol problems?

Yes. This does not mean they will develop an alcohol-related problem, but having a family history of alcohol-related problems is one of the factors that increases the risk. The degree of risk is related to:

- The closeness of the relative who has the alcohol-related problem
- The number of relatives involved

Knowing the family's health history can be important in making informed choices about drinking and the potential risks.

8. Can a person drink the same amount as they get older?

The older a person gets, the less well their body can 'handle' alcohol.

Changes in the body's makeup and metabolism, and increased use of medications as a person grows older, affect the way they process alcohol. Alcohol can increase the risk of falls, accidents while driving, and suicide in older people. Some medications, when used in combination with alcohol, can also further increase these risks, as well as reduce their effectiveness or increase side-effects.

Professional advice about alcohol related difficulties can be obtained from a GP and/or by going online to: National Drugs Campaign: http://www.drugs.health.gov.au/ (Choose the *Need Help* tab). This site has Australia-wide resources including Counselling Online details.

There are useful self-help options to be found in the book, *Taking Care of Yourself and Your Family: A Resource Book for Good Mental Health*, in the chapter titled: Alcohol. This chapter has lots of general information, and explores self-help options for alcohol reduction or cessation. There may be a copy in your local library. If not, go online to www.youcanhelppublishing.com

Caffeine

Caffeine is arguably the world's most widely consumed psychoactive substance, and it is commonly consumed regularly every day in workplaces because it is an effective psychostimulant. Despite its popularity, caffeine (mostly consumed through coffee drinking), has several negative affects you might want to consider, especially if you are a person who is experiencing stress, anxiety, or insomnia. Caffeine may appear innocuous because of its popularity, but it is a poor substitute for proper self-care.

As the stimulant found in coffee, caffeine is commonly consumed in the morning as a pick-me-up. The way it works is to stimulate production of the hormone adrenaline. This is normally a stress-triggered hormone that is intended to heighten your physical strength and alertness for a short period in response to a perceived threat. This is one feature of a much broader physiological activation referred to as the 'fight or flight response'. Release of adrenaline is marked by elevated heart rate, elevated blood pressure and heightened energy. This wide-ranging systemic activation of body organs is quite unhealthy if it is a daily chronic pattern. Also, though caffeine may deliver you a quick burst of energy, it may be followed by some degree of crash, marked by fatigue and irritability.

> Though caffeine may deliver you a quick burst of energy, it may be followed by some degree of crash, marked by fatigue and irritability.

It is worth mentioning here that some frequent consumers of caffeine, fool themselves into thinking that adrenaline fuelled energy is somehow a healthy and desirable state, one in which they are functioning at their best, including most creatively. However, functioning from a place of mindful well-slept calm is far superior to the artificial state of arousal, and without the negative health implications.

One of the problems with caffeine is that it has a long half-life, which means it stays in your blood stream a long time before being fully out of your system. Around 50% of the drug may be cleared from your body within 5-6 hours, but it may take up to a full day or more to fully eliminate it from your system.

Any caffeine in your bloodstream at bedtime may make it harder to get off to sleep, but will also disrupt the quality of your sleep by altering your sleep architecture, or the pattern of your sleep. It will reduce your rapid eye movement sleep (REM). After a disrupted sleep, you'll likely wake feeling tired. Drink coffee again to stimulate your system, and a vicious cycle begins to emerge. Sleep loss is cumulative, and even small nightly decreases can add up and disturb your daytime alertness and performance.

The direct effects of caffeine during the day, plus the added problem of caffeine related sleep deprivation can significantly add to the burden of stress and anxiety you may be experiencing, and will likely make it more difficult for you to manage strong emotions.

Caffeine can interact with some medications and herbal supplements. For example, some antibiotics can interfere with the breakdown of caffeine (which may increase the length of time it remains in your body), and may also amplify unwanted effects of caffeine. Medication prescribed to open bronchial airways may react with caffeine causing nausea, vomiting and heart palpitations. The common supplement Echinacea, used to assist with colds and other infections, may increase the concentration of caffeine in your blood and increase the likelihood of some of caffeine's unpleasant effects, including:

- Insomnia
- Nervousness
- Restlessness
- Irritability
- Stomach upset
- Fast heartbeat
- Muscle tremors

Curbing your caffeine habit

It is best not to abruptly cease or too rapidly decrease your caffeine intake because you may experience withdrawal symptoms, such as headaches, fatigue, irritability and nervousness. Best to cut down slowly over a couple of weeks. Perhaps start with the rule that you don't drink any caffeine containing beverage after mid-afternoon - preferably midday.

To change your caffeine habit more gradually, consider:

- *Cutting back.* But do it gradually. For example, drink smaller and less cups of coffee each day. Or avoid drinking caffeinated beverages late in the day. This will help your body get used to the lower levels of caffeine and lessen potential withdrawal effects.
- *Keeping tabs.* Start paying attention to how much caffeine you're getting from beverages and food. Read labels carefully. Even then, your estimate may be a little low because not all foods or drinks list caffeine. Chocolate, which has a small amount, doesn't.
- *Switching to decaffeinated.* Most decaffeinated beverages look and taste the same as their caffeinated counterparts, so they are good substitute.
- *Checking the bottle.* Even some over-the-counter pain relievers contain caffeine - as much as 130 mg of caffeine in one dose. Look for caffeine-free pain relievers instead.

Nicotine

Smoking is one of the leading preventable causes of death in Australian. And smoking doesn't only cause lung cancer, it causes 16 types of cancer. Tobacco smoke contains more than 7,000 chemicals, including over 70 carcinogens known to trigger cancer. Smoking is associated with impotence, heart attack, stroke, high blood pressure, emphysema, chronic bronchitis, diabetes, eye deterioration, dental and gum problems. Middle aged men who are long-term heavy smokers, have double the risk of aggressive prostate cancer. Recent research has found that smoking can alter your genes and leave a lasting effect on your DNA - making you vulnerable to cancer and other diseases.

Remember the Marlboro Man advertisements? They still feature on billboard advertising in developing countries. Well, the Marlboro man didn't get to ride off into the sunset, he died of lung cancer! Well, to be more exact, two of them did (a variety of men did the ads). Of the two that did die (that we know of), both became anti-smoking campaigners.

Doubtless you've heard all the warnings about tobacco and nicotine before. But did you know although most smokers report wanting to quit, others continue on their 'merry way' because of the belief that smoking provides them with mental health benefits. Moreover, evidence suggests that many regular smokers believe cigarettes alleviate emotional problems, feelings of depression, stress and anxiety, mood swings, and tension. Such views about smoking, of course, influence their preparedness to quit.

Well here is the irony: smokers who believe this are not only mistaken, but could likely experience improvement in their mental health by quitting the habit. Research published in the British Medical Journal showed that people who quit smoking experienced a significant drop in anxiety, depression and stress. This effect was true for both the general population of smokers and those with a diagnosed mental health difficulty. Quitting was found to be at least as effective for alleviating depression and anxiety as taking antidepressants. Those who quit also experienced an increase in both quality of life and positive emotion. This finding swiftly demolishes any myth that smoking can contribute to improved mental health; far from it, it undermines it, and is strongly contrary to self-care.

> Research published in the British Medical Journal showed that people who quit smoking experienced a significant drop in anxiety, depression and stress.

If you are a smoker, the single biggest thing you can do to improve your health is to quit. And you might just save your life as well. The benefits of quitting are almost immediate. With nicotine cleared from your system, your blood pressure will start to return to normal. Within a few days your lungs will function better, and exercise will become easier. Your sense of taste and smell will start to normalise. Within a year, your risk of lung cancer will reduce, and your risk of heart disease will be almost half that of someone who

> If you are a smoker, the single biggest thing you can do to improve your health is to quit. And you might just save your life as well.

keeps smoking. You will also stop putting those around you at risk.

There's no 'right' way to quit smoking. And no matter what you do, you'll still need to be determined and to work at it. Most smokers still try to throw the habit 'cold turkey', without any help. But getting some support, and maybe medication, can improve your odds of success. Your doctor may suggest Nicotine Replacement Therapy or some other form of medication to help with physical addiction, and re-establishing abstinence after a 'slip-up'. But physical cravings are only half of the equation; psychological attachment must also be tackled. That's why, for most people, a stop smoking program which provides personal support and follow-up is best. An excellent option is the free 24/7 QUITLINE on 13 18 48, offering a 12-week program.

No matter how long you have been smoking, it is well worth quitting. To plan on doing so, is a powerful act of power in taking control of your health and in your commitment to self-care.

Getting Enough Exercise to Stay Healthy

You've probably heard the warnings that Australians are becoming increasingly obese, and are becoming inactive at a faster rate than people of any other country. In fact, only about half of us get anything like the amount of exercise we need for good health. The good news is that we don't have to go in for heroics, becoming pavement-pounding joggers or perspiration drenched gym junkies, to get the minimum exercise needed for good health.

> The good news is that we don't have to go in for heroics, becoming pavement-pounding joggers or perspiration drenched gym junkies, to get the minimum exercise needed for good health.

Australia's Physical Activity and Sedentary Behaviour Guidelines point out that moderate daily exercise has important benefits for physical and mental health. It reduces the risk of many health problems, such as cardiovascular disease, type 2 diabetes, anxiety, depression, musculoskeletal problems, some cancers and unhealthy weight gain. Here are what the guidelines suggest:

The Physical Activity Guidelines recommend (for 18 - 65 year olds):

- Doing any physical activity is better than doing none. If you currently do no physical activity, start by doing some, and gradually build up to the recommended amount.
- Be active on most, preferably all, days every week.
- Accumulate 2½ to 5 hours (150 to 300 minutes) of *moderate intensity* physical activity or 1¼ to 2½ hours (75 to 150 minutes) of *vigorous intensity* physical activity, or an equivalent combination of both moderate and vigorous activities, each week.
- Do muscle strengthening activities at least 2 days each week.

Sedentary Behaviour Guidelines

- Minimise the amount of time spent in prolonged sitting.
- Break up long periods of sitting as often as possible.
- If you are unaccustomed to activity it's best to start gently (for example, by walking), without overexertion, and to gradually build up towards reaching recommended levels. Consult a health professional if you're unsure.

Even three 10-minute bouts of exercise each day will do, so long as it's of moderate intensity – which means it should cause a slight but noticeable increase in breathing and heart rate.

What kind of exercise is best? Well the choice is yours, but what's easy and doesn't require any equipment – except suitable footwear, is brisk walking. Of course, mowing the lawn, tennis, dancing, swimming, cycling and other forms of exercise are fine, so long as they elevate both your breathing and heart rate. You'll know you've got this about right if you can talk but not sing. If you also want to achieve fitness or avoid weight gain, then you'll have to work harder, by ramping up the pace to more vigorous exercise, through jogging, competitive sport, aerobics, or something comparable.

It's easy to kid ourselves that we are more active than we are, simply because we arrive home exhausted. But exhaustion is not the same as exertion. And, in fact, we might feel a good deal less tired if we got more exercise. It's also easy to make excuses not to exercise, the classic being: 'I just don't seem to have the time'. Well it's all a matter of priorities. How important is your health? Australians manage to watch an average of around two hours of television each day. Even if you don't, earmarking 30 minutes for exercise amongst other recreational activities represents only a small adjustment, and is a great investment in your health.

Remember, think of daily physical activity as an opportunity, not an inconvenience. Try to be active every day in as many ways as you can; regularity is vital. Build exercise into your daily routine. For extra health and fitness, get more exercise or make it more vigorous. If you have a medical condition, first get some advice from your doctor about the best form and level of exercise for you.

> Remember, think of daily physical activity as an opportunity, not an inconvenience.

You Are What You Eat

More than 60% of Australian adults are overweight or obese and the figure is rising. Being overweight is the biggest cause of diabetes, and is strongly linked to high cholesterol, and colorectal and gall bladder cancer. For men, it can be a killjoy in the trouser department too, because it increases the risk of impotence and infertility. It can also cause or worsen a potentially serious condition called sleep apnea, often resulting in chronic sleeplessness.

How much fat is too much fat? Is being thin necessarily healthy? To be fat and fit is probably better than to be thin and unfit. But the former is an unlikely combination. And saying: "I'm just big boned" or "There's more of me to love" won't wash either, when your heart gives out or you find yourself with diabetes.

The most recognised rule of thumb now is *waist size* (fat around your stomach), not weight; and *waist reduction*, rather than weight reduction. For every 1kg (2lbs) in weight that you shed, your waist will reduce by around 1cm. For men, fat stored around the stomach is a real health hazard. Reducing the size of your gut by 5-10cm can significantly improve your health.

> The most recognised rule of thumb now is waist size (fat around your stomach), not weight; and waist reduction, rather than weight reduction.

Forget the body beautiful stereotypes. Your ideal weight will be different to other peoples': that's just how you've been made. And your ideal weight will emerge only with proper diet and regular exercise.

What can you do to reduce your waist circumference? Forget the quick fix diets; they're a scam. You can lose weight rapidly with a diet, but the fat will probably return with a vengeance.

Rapid dieting gets your body thinking that you're entering a famine period, so it puts the brakes on burning calories - to save energy (thinking it's saving your life). That's why, when you start to eat properly again, chances are you'll put on more weight than you lost.

> Rapid dieting gets your body thinking that you're entering a famine period, so it puts the brakes on burning calories – to save energy (thinking it's saving your life).

Forget the heroics. A sensible diet and getting regular moderate exercise will, for the vast majority of people, slowly but surely fix the problem and deliver some real health benefits.

The question is: what should we be eating? Misleading food labelling and marketing, and the sometimes-conflicting messages we get about nutrition, haven't exactly made things clear or simple. Yet, despite all the confusion, the fundamentals of healthy eating have remained pretty much the same. Having said that, sugar is increasingly being seen as the culprit when it comes to obesity; an emphasis that somehow got lost with the focus on reducing dietary fat.

Some basic 'rules of thumb' are: moderation, variety, more plant-based foods, less fatty foods and sugar, and less rubbishy snacks. Eating a variety of foods in moderation will put you well on track:

combinations of low-fat dairy foods, lean meat and poultry, fish, vegetables, grainy bread, cereals, pasta, rice, beans and fruit are ideal.

By favouring cereals, pastas, grainy breads, fruit and vegetables, the fibre you get will help keep your cholesterol levels down, and give you some protection against bowel cancer.

> Some basic 'rules of thumb' are: moderation, variety, more plant-based foods, less fatty foods and sugar, and less rubbishy snacks.

Less sugary and fatty foods may help protect you against some major diseases like heart disease, cancer and diabetes. Always trim the fat off meat and poultry; avoid greasy fry-ups and tacky takeaways. Remember, the less fat you put *in* your stomach, the less you'll end up with *on* your stomach. Likewise, with sugar, less sugar, less unhealthy weight gain.

If you start reading food labels in supermarkets, you'll notice that though many foods in the health food section and on other shelves boast that they are healthy because they contain low or not fat, they are often high in sugar. Being a discerning consumer means spotting the marketing ploys, which are concerned with selling products not promoting your health.

As for snack foods, most of them have little nutritional value, so you have to be a bit more discerning. Try to avoid pastries with cream; limit pastries anyway – especially pies and sausage rolls (they are very high in fat). Go for small packets of fruit and nuts, rice snacks, muesli bars that are low in sugar and fat, and fruit (including dried fruit). If you eat cake, just have a small slice without cream. As for biscuits, go for those low in fat, but remember most are still high in sugar, something you shouldn't get too much of. If you have a sweet tooth, eat sweet things for a treat not for a meal.

Having a number of small meals each day is fine, but that doesn't mean adding lots of snacks to your regular three main meals.

Try eating more mindfully; become attentive to the flavours and textures of the food you eat instead of anticipating the next mouthful, and try eating at a slower pace. You'll find if you do, your appetite will be satisfied earlier, you'll eat less, and enjoy your food more. Still, you'll need to become sensitive to the internal

> Try eating more mindfully; become attentive to the flavours and textures of the food you eat instead of anticipating the next mouthful, and try eating at a slower pace.

appetite signals that are telling you that you have had enough. Listen for these and even if you haven't finished the serve you gave yourself, stop, and perhaps put the remainder away for a snack at another time.

Lastly, drink an adequate amount of water each day; it's vital for general health. Limit or eliminate cool drinks that are high in sugar or caffeine.

Remember, true healthcare reform doesn't begin in Canberra, but in your supermarket trolley, in your kitchen, and what you choose to eat while on the road!

Conflict: Learning to Manage the Unavoidable

Conflict is an inevitable and unavoidable part of working with and relating to others, which is why knowing how to deal with it constructively is so important. Conflict is a major source of stress for people who struggle to deal with it effectively, and it can easily spill over onto others that may be quite peripheral to it. Consequently, learning to manage conflict effectively, needs to be rated a high priority issue of self-care.

Conflict happens when we discover we disagree with another person about something - which can be a useful discovery if we make an effort to handle it in the right way. It often carries with it some strong feelings, which have the potential to either fuel a process of problem-solving, negotiation, and resolution - or more heated conflict!

> Conflict happens when we discover we disagree with another person about something – which can be a useful discovery if we make an effort to handle it in the right way.

Conflict that is quite minor may not need any kind of thoughtful process to resolve it. A little time may suffice; but how you feel about it and how your colleague or workmate feels may vary. It is safe to assume *that it is not safe to assume*, so asking is usually the best policy, and may be an important first step in learning how to approach conflict with appropriate assertiveness.

How we approach conflict determines its outcome

How conflict unfolds can very much depend on how *we decide* to approach it. The orientation and communication we choose in our approach to dealing with conflict in any given situation will likely significantly decide the outcome, even if the other party chooses not to be reasonable.

> How conflict unfolds can very much depend on how we decide to approach it.

For example, if our chosen approach is *other-centred* – acquiescent to the other person, using non-assertive language, the outcome will be a lose-win; afterwards leaving us feeling devalued and even angry. If our chosen approach is *self-centred* and our language is aggressive or manipulative, then the outcome will likely be a win-lose leaving the other person feeling devalued or angry, or that the conflict escalates and worsens. Alternatively, if our chosen disposition and approach is relationship-centred and our language is appropriately assertive or determined and committed to resolution, the outcome may turn out to be a win-win, or at worst (if the other person is unresponsive) the conflict may be primed for resolution on approaching it again in the near future.

It is important to understand the nature of relationships and why they are prone to conflict. Relationship is a *contested* space, one in which two people must find a compromise and negotiate to have their individual needs met, to be personally known, understood, and valued, despite being shaped by quite different personal histories and life experiences. Who we are as individuals is also ever changing as are our relationships. Both must remain flexible and able to adapt to shifting needs, beliefs, values, ideas and circumstances.

Given their sometimes-profound differences of personality, beliefs, experience, needs, dreams, likes and dislikes, human beings have an amazing capacity for intelligently and satisfactorily working things out and coexisting harmoniously. But conflict inevitably arises and must be worked through.

To reiterate: the way we approach conflict and the language we choose are vital ingredients of conflict resolution. Two other ingredients need to be added, first that we try to exercise empathy, a concerted effort to understand the other person's experience and perspective; second, that we don't have expectations of them that we largely fail to live up to or accommodate ourselves.

'Let us become the change we seek in the world'. Mahatma Gandhi

The positive and negative potential of conflict

Positive Potential

Dealt with well, conflict can have significantly positive outcomes for a relationship:

- People can get to know each other better: what they think, how they feel, and what is important to them
- Energy is released that can break through obstacles to allow necessary change and improvement occur
- It can clarify and 'clear up' false beliefs, misconceptions and false assumptions
- It can disperse tension and stress, and bring relief and calm
- It can help a relationship evolve, move forward, and strengthen

Negative Potential

Conflict that is dealt with poorly can have significantly negative consequences for a relationship:

- Conflict that is prolonged and not properly 'worked through' can be damaging for both people and the relationship
- Avoiding conflict can cause anger and resentment to build up and explode, causing damage disproportional to the issue that caused the conflict in the first place
- Suppression of conflict prevents opportunities for individuals to make the changes and adjustments necessary in a relationship, and to stay 'connected,' when faced with the inevitable emergence of differences and different needs
- The more poorly conflict is handled, the more trivial will be the things that trigger it again and the more habitual conflict will likely become
- Conflict left unresolved can cause growing confusion, exaggeration, and feelings of powerlessness, helplessness, and anger

Working with and through conflict

Working with and through conflict means using it to try and achieve a positive and constructive outcome, rather than merely the cessation of conflict.

Conflict resolution is about working together to find a solution that doesn't leave either of you feeling cheated or the loser. The solution you arrive at needs to leave both of you sufficiently satisfied not to want to harbour ill-will, annoyance or resentment. It will need to leave you feeling heard, listened to and respected. The decisive test will be whether any residual feelings activate again, and whether you feel the need to complain to others about the outcome or about your experience.

> Conflict resolution is about working together to find a solution that doesn't leave either of you feeling cheated or the loser.

Some statements of disposition

- I will remain calm and respectful of the other person's experience and viewpoint
- I will try and appreciate their point of view
- I will not try and win but will aim for a compromise that both of us are comfortable with
- I will not be overbearing or manipulative, and will be patient and respectful in our communication
- I will say how I feel about the issue of contention without laying blame
- I will abstain from 'roping in' other issues that are not pertinent to the conflict
- I will abstain from any criticism of the other person's point of view, and will not discount her/his feelings
- I will ask the other person is he/she would be prepared to help work out a solution with me that is agreeable and feels OK for both of us

What if things can't be worked out?

Sometimes, with the best will in the world, it just doesn't seem possible to resolve a conflict ourselves - perhaps because feelings are too strong, or the issues are very difficult or complicated. A third person from outside the situation can be very helpful in providing some objectivity, assisting us to think more broadly and creatively, and perhaps to making better sense of what we want, mean, feel, and can reasonably expect of each other.

Because conflict resolution requires time, energy, honesty, and vulnerability, it pays to try to find the right person to help 'first time around' if possible, rather than having to go over the matter again with someone else. To begin with, you may consider avoiding language like mediation (which may suggest a less than amicable situation) and prefer 'having someone help us work through a difficulty'.

Meditation for in the Workplace

When you hear the word *meditation* what kind of image comes to mind: someone who has become a devotee of an Eastern philosophy, or a group run by a church or community group in your neighbourhood? Perhaps for you the word meditation implies religion, pop psychology, or new ageism? Being cautious about fads and trends is always a good idea, but in this case, it would be a real pity to, 'throw the baby out with the bathwater'. If you dig beneath the surface a little with meditation, you'll discover it has a growing and quite robust evidence base; it can have outcomes that are excellent for your mental health and wellbeing.

If you dig beneath the surface a little with meditation, you'll discover it has a growing and quite robust evidence base; it can have outcomes that are excellent for your mental health and wellbeing. Its principles are simple to grasp and can be practised without signing up to any spiritual or religious beliefs. Meditation can stand alone without any reliance on religion or spirituality. It doesn't even emanate exclusively from the East, it has been practised in one form or another since time immemorial.

The value of meditation for self-care and cultivating self-compassion is now widely acknowledged. Using modern scientific techniques and instruments, such as fMRI and EEG which can directly observe brain physiology and neural activity in living subjects, meditation has been shown to influence changes in brain function and structure. For example, it has been shown to reduce the activity of the brain activation centre responsible for triggering the flight or fight response and setting the tone of emotional experience. There are many studies that highlight mental and physical health benefits of meditation and one of its more recent 'relatives', *mindfulness*.

Studies have also established that meditation practices can create changes in grey matter concentration in brain regions involved in learning and memory processes, emotion regulation, self-referential processing, and perspective taking. It has also been found to be effective in resolving mental health difficulties of anxiety and depression.

It is well known that rumination (going over and over thoughts and experience in our mind) and worry, contribute to mental health difficulties of stress, depression, and anxiety. Meditation has been found to be an effective retardant of and management strategy for rumination.

> Meditation has been found to be an effective retardant of and management strategy for rumination.

Meditation has also been found to contribute to a more coherent sense of self and self-identity, enhanced memory, and mental clarity. It can help you function calmly, at a healthy pace, and with an awareness that can bring a whole lot more quality and flavour to your day. And yes, it has immediate relevance to the demanding 'rough and tumble' of your workaday life.

The following are some basic principles of meditation you may like to try. Forget about any notion of a hierarchy of steps or attainment, these principles are interrelated. They take practice and require gentleness; practice, referring to frequent use – until they've become 'second nature'; gentleness, referring to being in every way gentle and patient with yourself, and your practice. What is presented here are principles of meditation to support your endeavour of self-care. You can of course extend your understanding of meditation through your own reading; many books are available on the subject.

Becoming anchored in a place of calm

The best way to start your day is first to anchor yourself in a place of calm. And by *start* is meant before you begin thinking about your day, using your mobile device, giving direction to children, or embarking on any kind of task that puts you deeply into you mind and its thoughts. The best way to end your day while readying yourself for sleep, is also to anchor yourself in a place of calm again. This can be done using a simple relaxation technique, but remember this needs to be approached with gentleness and patience, and in a way, that is rhythmic and respectful of your body.

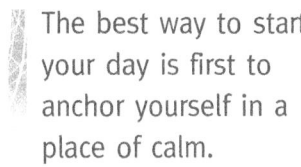

The best way to start your day is first to anchor yourself in a place of calm.

- *Breathe in slowly and fully through your nose.* Make sure your shoulders are down and relaxed. In this exercise, your stomach should expand, but your chest should rise very little. So, if you want, you can place one hand on your stomach and the other on your chest so you can feel how you are breathing.
- *Exhale slowly through your mouth.* As you breathe air out, purse your lips slightly, but make sure you keep your tongue and jaw relaxed. You may hear a soft 'whooshing' sound as you exhale. That's good, listen for that sound every time you practice and learn to value it as the sound of relaxation.
- *Repeat this breathing exercise for several minutes.* Make your outgoing breath as long and smooth as you can. The outgoing breath is the key to relaxation so give it your full attention and practice breathing out in a long slow controlled way and you will quickly feel the benefit.
- All the time *listen to and learn to focus on your breath*, because this will help train your attention.

Very likely, at least at first, you will lose your sense of calm several times during your working day. After a while, and with practice you will notice this quite soon after it has happened. When it does, simply, use the relaxation technique and anchor yourself in a place of calm again.

Slowing your motion

Anchoring yourself in a place of calm is important, but equally so is knowing how to best sustain that calm for as long as possible. This can be accomplished by *slowing your motion*. This is different from *slow motion*, it means instead slowing down your physical motion in all ways enough to maintain your sense of calm, but not so much (as with slow motion) that others will think it strange. On observing your movements, they will merely think you are calm and going about your day sedately.

This is the simplest and yet most sophisticated principle you can practice and learn. It will accomplish several things at once. It will quite quickly cultivate your awareness of the present moment and of your senses; it will enable you to notice things and experience them more fully. It will also train your attention - your ability to focus your mind in the present rather than in the past or the future. It will enable you to become mindful, which will result in a positive qualitative shift in your experience of almost everything, a change in your consciousness.

This is a hugely valuable principle especially if you are an intense, introverted, or anxious person. It is also of great benefit if you must engage in public speaking or perform some other task that normally causes you to experience a spike in stress.

> This is a hugely valuable principle especially if you are an intense, introverted, or anxious person.

Though usually best used with first anchoring yourself in a place of calm, in time, you may also find it is useful to practice on its own. If you notice early enough that your motion has sped up again, you can simply slow things down. If necessary, take a couple of minutes to anchor yourself in a place of calm and then commence again *slowing your motion*.

Should you think to yourself, 'I don't have time in my busy job or role to slow down', then think again. Not only is it fully possible to slow your motion no matter how demanding or busy your role (with very few exceptions), you will also function more effectively, use less energy, will make less mistakes, will be generally more productive, and will learn to operate out of a place of *thoughtful deliberate calm* rather than adrenalin fuelled phreneticism. As soon as you begin functioning frantically, important

> Slowing your motion then, represents an economy of calm. Functioning phrenetically is a false economy.

thinking functions of the left prefrontal cortex part of your brain begin to switch off, and your body is assaulted by hormones that are potentially toxic to your health. Slowing your motion then, represents an *economy of calm.* Functioning phrenetically is a false economy.

There is one more thing to mention here: the *philanthropy of calm*. All of us know how contagious stress is; if you work with a group of people and one of them is quite anxious and stressed, it tends to be catching, and in time the whole group may become more stressed. The same is true of calm. If you can attain and maintain calm, you will probably influence the rest of the group which will *response match* (just as with stress). Used consciously in the workplace this principle can positively transform not only the conditions affecting people's physical and mental health, it can transform the quality of relationships, reduce conflict, and improve productivity and creativity.

Training your attention

As we have just discussed, slowing your motion can help cultivate attention and awareness. Attention and awareness are keys to improving our quality of life and more specifically the quality of our experience. This can be easily understood if we consider one of the most common features reported by people suffering the effects of depression and anxiety: *rumination* - going over and over thoughts and experiences in one's mind. In the case of depression, rumination takes the form of a preoccupation with memories, with things in the past. With anxiety, rumination takes the form of a preoccupation with fearful anticipations of the future - imagining or predicting what could happen, might happen, and will happen. Both kinds of rumination can lead to a decline in mental health. Both have to do with not living in the present moment, in fact, both sacrifice the present moment and all that could be more fully experienced in it, for a past that is done and is unchangeable, or a future that may not, and often does not turn out as fear might predict. Training attention (which also brings awareness - a new kind of *noticing* and a fuller and more meaningful experience), is a powerful antidote to rumination.

> With anxiety, rumination takes the form of a preoccupation with fearful anticipations of the future – imagining or predicting what could happen, might happen, and will happen.

Another benefit of training attention is that sometimes-overwhelming emotions can be more quickly smoothed out' and 'tamed' so that they don't dominate our experience and leave us either miserable or overstimulated. When we can live more fully in the present moment and attend to what is in front of us, to the exclusion of run-away thoughts, we can become progressively masters of our own emotions. With the awareness that flourishes with attention also comes the capacity for being much more conscious of our emotions as they arise. It can enable us to 'step back from them' acknowledge them, notice their nature, and the thoughts that might accompany them. This can give us the choice to allow or disallow their escalation.

> With the awareness that flourishes with attention also comes the capacity for being much more conscious of our emotions as they arise.

The effects of training our attention on our brain can be profound in other ways, parts of our brain that set or contribute to regulating our emotion experience have their neural pathways modified, so that we tend to recover more quickly from painful emotions, and experience less unwanted and unnecessary 'fight or flight' activation and physiological arousal. Meditation and attention training have been found to alter grey matter density in a number of regions of the brain. As you will have gathered by now, meditation is not merely some kind of religious practice, it is a set of evidence based and accessible principles, which if practiced regularly, can change our brain 'wiring' and the way we experience our lives.

Simple ways to train your attention include:

- *Noticing ordinary everyday things, beginning at home*

Isolate an ordinary routine activity like shaving, bathing, brushing your teeth, ironing, washing dishes, making breakfast, and become attentive to every aspect and nuance of what you are doing. Being a routine activity, there will be lots of scope to practice and for this to become a ritualised way of training your attention every day. This is a form of meditation: deciding to be attentive, noticing, growing in awareness. This will be much easier if you also slow the process down a little, by *slowing your motion*.

Once you sense your capacity of attentiveness developing (you'll know because you will notice your awareness developing too), extend this practice to another regular activity like cooking, or a routine maintenance task or something else of your choice. With this practice happening at home, you can then start to become attentive to activities in your work day. Overall, you will start to experience what it means to live in the present moment. If you become stressed with a work demand, take a couple of minutes to anchor yourself in a place of calm, slow your motion, and continue your day again.

Remember, this should all be done with gentleness and patience. If you approach it aggressively or sternly, progress in that moment will 'grind to a halt'. Slowly, gently, deliberately practice this principle.

- *Set a reminder on your mobile device to stop for a couple of minutes every hour or two hours*

You can download a Mind Bell application free, and can set it so that you are reminded to stop for a couple of minutes and to be especially attentive to whatever it is you are doing, or to concentrate on the rhythm of your breathing - each inward and outward breath. When the reminder sounds, treat it with the same priority as you might something else of importance that you wouldn't ignore and would gladly, stop to attend to.

Alternatively, just stop periodically throughout your day and notice what is in front of you for a couple of minutes, in a gently nuanced way.

- *Take time out to become attentive to your breathing*

This is a meditative practice and cultivator of attention common in nearly all ancient traditions of meditation. Simply stop for a few minutes throughout your day, with your eyes open or closed pay attention to your breathing (each inward and outward breath), and the rhythm of your breathing. Following your breathing shouldn't alter its rhythm, because you are observing it gently and respectfully. This is a practice that can be used at almost any time during your working day.

> Simply stop for a few minutes throughout your day, with your eyes open or closed pay attention to your breathing (each inward and outward breath), and the rhythm of your breathing.

- *Take time out to observe your physical sensations, thoughts, and emotions*

A popular practice of meditation is to take some time to close your eyes and observe the sensations you may be experiencing in your body, beginning with the soles of your feet right up to your head and scalp. Then, shift your attention to the emotion content of your experience, which, though always present, may sometimes be quite subtle. Then, shift your attention to observing the thoughts that pass across you mind.

In addition to training your attention this practice can give you a sense of being less identified or enmeshed with these elements of your experience, so that you can be more of an observer and 'stage manager'. It can enable you at times when your thoughts are unruly or unhelpful, or your emotions are strong and have potential to be overwhelming, to be able to step back a little and not be carried away or dominated by them.

- *Use your daily walks to cultivate attention*

Another easy way to help cultivate your capacity of attention is to use your daily walks (if that is how you gain some exercise). Just find a simple object in the distance to fix your attention on, and stay with that object remaining attentive to its form until you arrive. On your return, repeat this practice again focusing on a different object. This doesn't mean you can't be aware of where you are walking, nor does it prevent you from being careful with your footsteps. An alternative practice, is to observe and remain attentive to the rhythm of your breathing as you walk.

> Just find a simple object in the distance to fix your attention on, and stay with that object remaining attentive to its form until you arrive.

Responding to distractions

Perhaps you have stopped for a few minutes to notice more fully what is in front of you, what you are doing, following the rhythm of your breathing, or to observe sensations in your body? Maybe you have decided to notice the thoughts passing across your mind, or emotions present in your experience? Either way, there will inevitably be distracting thoughts that tend to lead you off in other directions and get you pondering all manner of other things.

Distractions are normal, natural, and inevitable, including for meditation veterans. They are your friend not your enemy, because each time you gently draw your attention back to the present moment and what you have decided to focus on, you are the same time retraining you brain and your mind in the practice of attention rather than dispersion, meaningful awareness rather than randomness and reverie. It is vital you understand this relationship, and that gentleness is essential in drawing away from distractions and paying attention again.

Choose not to allow situations or other people to pressure you into relinquishing your calm

There will always be other people who choose to be phrenetic and frenzied who will try and conscript you into their pace and adrenaline driven approach to a task or to their day. There will always be situations that try to do likewise – situations usually of other people's making that simply don't fit with the healthier pace and way of doing things you have chosen. Two things to note here are: if you are practising calm and training your attention, you *will* notice when someone or something is pressuring you to relinquish your calm. You have a choice to make, and, reminding yourself of the *economy of calm*, can choose to retain and not relinquish your calm and composure. If you must respond to someone stressfully urging you to move at their pace, you could respond by saying something like: 'I'd rather approach this thoughtfully and calmly', or, 'I think we can accomplish this better if we slow things down a little and approach this calmly'.

> There will always be other people who choose to be phrenetic and frenzied who will try and conscript you into their pace and adrenaline driven approach to a task or to their day.

Choose not to be pulled in too many directions

There is a growing consensus that so called 'multi-tasking', rather than being a clever thing to do, may be taking its toll on our physical and mental health, and lowering our work quality and efficiency. Maybe there is some truth in the Roman proverb: *The man who chases two rabbits catches none*? Certainly, any behaviour that is constantly so at odds with us being in the present moment and attentive to what we are doing, will have its consequences. So, what does being attentive mean in a work environment that seems to hurl so many demands at us at the same time?

The problem (in most cases) leads back to us. Most often we can make choices in our work day that allow us to be more focused on less things at any one time. When you start your day, instead of immediately launching into several tasks, why not begin with one: prioritising your day? Do you need to read emails as they arrive across the day? Do you need to be available always to take phone calls? Is it helpful (or appropriate) to be checking personal emails or Facebook on your phone during working hours? It may well be that just by acknowledging that multi-tasking is undesirable in most circumstances, that you can plan work tasks and demands in a more manageable sequence that permits you to be attentive to each.

References

16 cancers – Quit Victoria. (2016). *Quit.org.au*. http://www.quit.org.au/reasons-to-quit/health-risks-of-smoking/16-cancers

Abigail, R. & Cahn, D. (2011). *Managing conflict through communication* (1st ed.). Boston, MA: Allyn & Bacon.

Australian Dietary Guidelines (2013). *National Health and Medical Research Council*. (2013). *Nhmrc.gov.au*. https://www.nhmrc.gov.au/guidelines-publications/n55

Australian Institute of Family Studies. (2017). *Australian Institute of Family Studies*. https://aifs.gov.au/

Alcohol and other drugs (AIHW). (2017). *Aihw.gov.au*. http://www.aihw.gov.au/alcohol-and-other-drugs/

Beaumont, E. & Hollins-Martin, C. (2015). A narrative review exploring the effectiveness of compassion focused therapy. *Counselling Psychology Review*, *30*(1), 21-32.

Betterhealth.vic.gov.au. (2016). https://www.betterhealth.vic.gov.au/

BJPsych Advances. (2017). *Apt.rcpsych.org*. http://apt.rcpsych.org/

Blomberg, K. & Sahlberg-Blom, E. (2007). Closeness and distance: a way of handling difficult situations in daily care. *Journal of Clinical Nursing*, *16*(2), 244-254. http://dx.doi.org/10.1111/j.1365-2702.2005.01503.x

CDC Works 24/7. (2016). *Centers for Disease Control and Prevention*. https://www.cdc.gov/

Crescentini, C. & Capurso, V. (2015). Mindfulness meditation and explicit and implicit indicators of personality and self-concept changes. *Frontiers in Psychology*, *6*. http://dx.doi.org/10.3389/fpsyg.2015.00044

Crescentini, C., Matiz, A., & Fabbro, F. (2015). Improving personality/character traits in individuals with alcohol dependence: the influence of mindfulness-oriented meditation. *Journal of Addictive Diseases*, *34*(1), 75-87. http://dx.doi.org/10.1080/10550887.2014.991657

Department of Health. Australia's Physical Activity and Sedentary Behaviour Guidelines. (2014). http://www.health.gov.au/internet/main/publishing.nsf/content/health-pubhlth-strateg-phys-act-guidelines

DrugInfo. *Facts about Alcohol & Drug Prevention – DrugInfo*. (2017). *Druginfo.adf.org.au*. http://www.druginfo.adf.org.au/

Figley, C. (2013). *Figley Institute. Figleyinstitute.com*. http://www.figleyinstitute.com/

Frankl, V. (2006). *Man's search for meaning* (1st ed.). Boston: Beacon Press.

Gilbert, P. (2005). Evolution and depression: issues and implications. *Psychological Medicine*, *36*(03), 287. http://dx.doi.org/10.1017/s0033291705006112

Goyal, M., Singh, S., Sibinga, E., Gould, N., Rowland-Seymour, A., & Sharma, R. et al. (2014). Meditation programs for psychological stress and well-being. *JAMA Internal Medicine*, *174*(3), 357. http://dx.doi.org/10.1001/jamainternmed.2013.13018

Healthdirect.gov.au. (2017) https://www.healthdirect.gov.au/

Hölzel, B., Carmody, J., Evans, K., Hoge, E., Dusek, J., & Morgan, L. et al. (2009). Stress reduction correlates with structural changes in the amygdala. *Social Cognitive and Affective Neuroscience*, *5*(1), 11-17. http://dx.doi.org/10.1093/scan/nsp034

Hölzel, B., Carmody, J., Vangel, M., Congleton, C., Yerramsetti, S., Gard, T., & Lazar, S. (2011). Mindfulness practice leads to increases in regional brain gray matter density.

Psychiatry Research: Neuroimaging, *191*(1), 36- 43. http://dx.doi.org/10.1016/j.pscychresns.2010.08.006

Hubble, M., Duncan, B., & Miller, S. (1999). *The heart & soul of change* (1st ed.). Washington, DC: American Psychological Association.

Jung, C. (1933). *Modern man in search of a soul* (1st ed.). New York: Harcourt, Brace & World.

Jung, C. & Jarrett, J. (1998). *Jung's seminar on Nietzsche's Zarathustra* (1st ed.). Princeton, N.J.: Princeton University Press.

Laing, R. (1969). *The divided self* (1st ed.). New York: Pantheon Books.

Leaviss, J. & Uttley, L. (2014). Psychotherapeutic benefits of compassion-focused therapy: an early systematic review. *Psychological Medicine*, *45*(05), 927-945. http://dx.doi.org/10.1017/s0033291714002141

Mairean, C., Cimpoesu, D., Turliuc, M.N. (2014). The effects of traumatic situations on emergency medicine practitioners. *Revista de Cercetare si Interventie Sociala*, *44*, 279-290.

Mark, G., Iqbal, S., Czerwinski, M., Johns, P., & Sano, A. (2016). Neurotics can't focus. *Proceedings of the 2016 CHI Conference on Human Factors in Computing Systems - CHI 16*. http://dx.doi.org/10.1145/2858036.2858202

Mayo Clinic. (2017). *Mayoclinic.org*. http://www.mayoclinic.org/patient-care-and-health-information

Merlin, M. (2003). COVER ARTICLE: Archaeological evidence for the tradition of psychoactive plant use in the old world. *Economic Botany*, *57*(3), 295-323. http://dx.doi.org/10.1663/0013-0001(2003)057 [0295:aeftto]2.0.co;2

Neff, K., Kirkpatrick, K., & Rude, S. (2007). Self-compassion and adaptive psychological functioning. *Journal of Research in Personality*, *41*(1), 139-154. http://dx.doi.org/10.1016/j.jrp.2006.03.004

Newell, J. & MacNeil, G. (2010). Professional burnout, vicarious trauma, secondary traumatic stress, and compassion fatigue: a review of theoretical terms, risk factors, and preventive methods for clinicians and researchers. *Best Practice in Mental Health Summer 2010*, *6*(2), 57. http://connection.ebscohost.com/c/articles/60132515/professional-burnout-vicarious-trauma-secondary-traumatic-stress-compassion-fatigue-review-theoretical-terms-risk-factors-preventive-methods-clinicians-researchers

Ophir, E., Nass, C., & Wagner, A. (2009). Cognitive control in media multitaskers. *Proceedings of The National Academy of Sciences*, *106*(37), 15583-15587. http://dx.doi.org/10.1073/pnas.0903620106

Powell, J. (1969). *Why am I afraid to tell you who I am?* (1st ed.). Chicago: Argus Communications.

Sansbury, B., Graves, K., & Scott, W. (2014). Managing traumatic stress responses among clinicians: individual and organisational tools for self-care. *Trauma*, *17*(2), 114-122. http://dx.doi.org/10.1177/1460408614551978

Sodeke-Gregson, E., Holttum, S., & Billings, J. (2013). Compassion satisfaction, burnout, and secondary traumatic stress in UK therapists who work with adult trauma clients. *European Journal of Psychotraumatology*, *4*(0). http://dx.doi.org/10.3402/ejpt.v4i0.21869

Stephen, K. (2014). *A Game Free Life* (1st ed.). Self-Published.

Supporting adult survivors of childhood trauma & abuse. (2017). *Blueknot.org.au*. http://www.blueknot.org.au/

Taylor, G., McNeill, A., Girling, A., Farley, A., Lindson-Hawley, N., & Aveyard, P. (2014). Change in mental health after smoking cessation: systematic review and meta-analysis. *BMJ*, *348*(feb13 1), g1151-g1151. http://dx.doi.org/10.1136/bmj.g1151

The Wendt Center for Loss & Healing. *Rekindling hope. Rebuilding lives.* (2017). *Wendtcenter.org*. http://www.wendtcenter.org/

Tillett, G. (1999). *Resolving conflict* (1st ed.). South Melbourne: Oxford University Press.

Zimbardo, P. & Boyd, J. (2009). *The time paradox* (1st ed.). New York: Free Press.

For a full list of resources or to place an order online, please see our website:
www.youcanhelp.com.au

you can help
PUBLISHING

We are careful to select themes and subjects that are of most importance and practical value for potential readers

These publications are from Australia's leading author of mental health promotion literature, Dr John Ashfield, PhD.

Mental Health for Men

Common Problems ~ Practical Solutions

Health *for* Gents

Vital Topics
~ *of* ~
Men's Health

SUPPORTING
Men in **Distress**

A Resource for Women

TEENAGERS
AND SELF HARM

Preventing Suicide in Indigenous Communities

Essential reading for those who aim to make a difference

Dictionary for End of Life Care

The language of medicine and medications made simple

For non-medical staff, carers and volunteers

Doing Psychotherapy With Men

Practicing ethical psychotherapy and counselling with men

Taking Care of Yourself and Your Family

Available at:
Website: www.youcanhelp.com.au Email: info@youcanhelp.com.au

www.ingramcontent.com/pod-product-compliance
Lightning Source LLC
Chambersburg PA
CBHW071414040426
42444CB00009B/2245